PREACHING
THROUGH THE YEAR

David Steel

SAINT ANDREW PRESS

EDINBURGH

First published in 1980 by
JOHN KNOX PRESS, USA

Revised and reformatted edition 1998
SAINT ANDREW PRESS
121 George Street, Edinburgh EH2 4YN

ISBN 0 7152 0760 1

British Library Cataloguing in Publication Data
A catalogue record for this book
is available from the British Library.

ISBN 0715207601

The publisher gratefully acknowledges
the financial assistance of **The Drummond Trust.**

Design concept by Mark Blackadder.
Typeset by Neil Gowans.
Printed and bound in Great Britain by
Redwood Books, Trowbridge, Wiltshire

Contents

To Sheila

Foreword

by the
REVD DR JAMES DAVISON PHILIPS

IN 1977 Dr and Mrs David Steel came to Columbia Theological Seminary in Metropolitan Atlanta to begin a remarkable ministry with students and faculty. It continued for six years, providing a semester a year for us.

A joint invitation with Peachtree Presbyterian Church of Atlanta, the largest Church in the Presbyterian Church, USA, gave Dr Steel two opportunities. At the Peachtree Church he was 'Theologian in Residence' and taught almost weekly, various adult classes and groups there in the areas of Bible, Theology and Ecumenics.

However, as President of Columbia Theological Seminary, I acknowledge a great debt of gratitude to Dr and Mrs Steel for their presence and participation there. In addition to teaching courses for prospective pastors in such areas as 'Preaching through the Year', he built lasting relationships with graduates and ministers throughout the Southeastern United States, and overseas students as well. Numerous preaching missions were the result.

The experiences of Dr and Mrs Steel in overseas ministry in Kenya, in pastoral experiences at Linlithgow, Scotland, and as a leader in the Church of Scotland as Moderator, was of great value in his teaching and counselling.

Mrs Steel entered fully into the life of the Campus Community during these terms and was greatly admired and appreciated. The Steels occupied a faculty apartment and shared many of their meals in the Refectory. This led to opportunities for friendship and counselling that many treasure today. They were a much appreciated influence in varied Campus activities.

The second edition of *Preaching through the Year* will, as did the first, be helpful and instructive to ministers in many and varied situations. I have found it so, personally, and am pleased that it is being published in a second edition.

REVD DR JAMES DAVISON PHILIPS
President Emeritus
COLUMBIA THEOLOGICAL SEMINARY
DECATUR, GA USA

Preface

THE first edition of *Preaching through the Year* was published in 1980 by the John Knox Press (now part of Westminster/John Knox Press) in America and Saint Andrew Press in Scotland. Unfortunately, the preface for that edition was lost in the post and the book was published without one.

I now have the opportunity to express my appreciation of the kindness and support of the highly regarded Columbia Theological College, Decatur, Atlanta, where for six years I lectured in the Spring or Fall term in my retirement after forty years of ministry in Scotland and Africa.

President Davison Philips and my colleagues and the staff were unfailingly helpful and encouraging. My wife Sheila and I enjoyed the fine suite for visiting lecturers, the campus, and the meals in the dining hall, which we shared with students and staff. In this way we got to know less formally both staff and students – some becoming friends for life. The students in the lecture room were attentive and appreciative.

The publication of *Preaching through the Year* was initiated by Professor John Leith of Union Theological Seminary, Virginia, one of America's most distinguished divinity scholars. I have been a guest in his home on two occasions when, at his request, I delivered a lecture at Union. He invited me again, but owing to pressure of work at Columbia I had to decline. He enquired about the subject of my work for Columbia, and I gave him over the phone an outline of the lectures on 'Preaching through the Year'.

I did not know that John Knox Press was publishing his notable book on *Reformed Tradition*, nor that he had spoken to them about the subject of my work and suggested they might be interested. The John Knox Press contacted me and asked if they might see some of my lectures, and, when I asked why, they told me of Professor Leith's suggestion. I gave them three lectures I had already delivered, but protested that they were not written for publication but to be spoken and would require some revision before publication. The revision was done and Sheila retyped all the lectures as I revised them. They were given to John Knox Press before I returned to Scotland and were dedicated to her with my inexpressible love and gratitude. The dedication was lost in the post with the original preface.

The book was well received both in America and Scotland – Saint Andrew Press published a co-edition with John Knox Press. It has now been out of print in both countries for twelve years. In these twelve years a new generation of ministers have begun their ministry. In both countries, also, there is an increase of auxiliary ministers, readers and lay people generally, who seek ways of learning to understand and express something of the range and depth of the Christian Faith in the Christian Year and suggestions as to the appropriate Word on various occasions.

I am much indebted to my publishers for their advice and generous support. This revised edition goes out with the hope and prayer that it may be of some help in what is an awesome privilege and responsibility – preaching through the year.

DAVID STEEL 1998

Introduction

IT was in 1953 that I first visited America. At that time I was Church of Scotland minister of St Andrew's Church, Nairobi and of the Parish of East Africa. This meant general responsibility for the spiritual welfare of expatriates who wished to avail themselves of my ministry, who were settlers or temporary residents in the three territories of Kenya, Uganda, and Tanganyika. A very considerable number of those expatriates were Scots. I was also a member of Mission Council and, with my missionary colleagues, shared responsibility for the evangelistic, educational, and medical work which the Church of Scotland undertook in partnership with the Presbyterian Church of East Africa.

It was an exciting time. In my first tour of four years, which came to an end in 1953, we had built a great new St Andrew's Church, we had seen the beginning of the union between the two wings, black and white, of the Presbyterian Church of East Africa, a union which came to pass in 1956. I had been permanent Moderator of the white wing of the Church and a leader in the union movement. I should make clear that we had no racial or colour bar. There were members of many colours and races, but the majority were white and from a variety of reformed churches. I had been Chairman of the Christian Council of Kenya, which was sometimes a wonderful fellowship and sometimes an uneasy alliance of British and American church and missionary societies and agencies: Episcopalian, Presbyterian, Methodist, Baptist, Independent, and the Salvation Army. In addition, there was Mau Mau, a situation of civil war and bloody cruelty, in which the Church had to exercise leadership; which demanded holy boldness, but which was also, all the time, both delicate and dangerous.

It was towards the end of four such exciting but hard years that I received a letter from the relevant assembly committee of the Church of Scotland informing me that I was coming on leave for six months – which I knew – and that I had been nominated to the British Council of Churches as one of the exchange preachers to go to America for two months and to be at the disposal of the National Council of Churches there. That I did not know – the news was not welcome. I was desperately tired. My weight was down to 112 pounds. I knew I would have to spend some of my six months' leave trying to inform the Church and the public about the complicated situation in Church and State in Kenya in particular and in Africa in general. And as for the rest, I wanted some time to read and to think and, above all, to go fishing! But it was not to be. As a soldier of Christ I am a man under authority. The worm wriggled, but he was hooked, and I had to go. I have been hooked ever since. I have returned again and again to America. Never again have I gone reluctantly. I have always been stimulated by the vitality of the Church in America and have enjoyed the fellowship of its saints and scholars. I have experienced the generous hospitality of America, and I have been astonished at the sometimes undeserved reputation which anyone speaking in an American church or theological seminary with a Scottish accent has for theological wisdom and pulpit eloquence. But it is nice to be at the receiving end of such generous if sometimes uncritical judgments.

The judgments, however, are not always uncritical. On that first visit to America I preached at Bryn Mawr. The next day, Monday, I was taken for a game of golf by the senior minister who had conducted the service. He paid me the compliment of saying that the sermon I had preached was what they looked for from the exchange preacher from Scotland – a text, an exposition, a sermon with straightforward theological content. He then said:

'We don't always get what we want and what we need. Would you tell your fellow Scots not to come here with what they think are their three best sermons, which are mere pyrotechnic displays, which may entertain but do not teach …. That kind of thing,' he concluded, 'we can do much better than you can.' It is a lesson which I accept and have passed on. They look to us for a contribution to biblical and theological preaching.

On one of my subsequent visits to America I served for three months as a member of the multi-ministerial team at Montview Boulevard Presbyterian Church, Denver, Colorado, under the leadership of Dr Arthur Miller, a former Moderator of the United Presbyterian Church in the USA. Towards the end of my three months I was asked by Dr Miller and the ministerial team if I would give them, at our last weekly session, a critique of Montview, which we would spend the morning discussing. I demurred on the grounds that I wanted to retain the friendship which I had so much appreciated. But they insisted.

I could and did say many complimentary things about a very fine ministerial team supported by first-class officers and leaders of a multitude of organisations for people, from the cradle to the grave, each with its well thought-out program and syllabus. All of this was housed and accommodated in a splendid modern custom-built plant which, though commonplace in America, was beyond the wildest dreams of any Church of Scotland minister. At the centre of it all was, very properly, the sanctuary, a fine neo-gothic church, with seats for a thousand people and regularly attended by a loyal congregation of that many or more at each of the two morning services.

And it was at this point that I made my main criticism. There in the sanctuary you had, Sunday by Sunday, by far the largest gathering for worship and for instruction in the faith once delivered to the saints. And there, there was a complete absence of program or of syllabus. There was, therefore, no thought-out system, no plan, no unity within the service of praise or prayers, lessons or sermon, no systematic teaching, not even a loose and flexible pattern of preaching or theme. 'Every man did that which was right in his own eyes,' and I felt that thereby a great opportunity was perhaps being missed. I had been asked by Dr Miller, before I left Scotland, if I would preach on the first Sunday after Easter – which was to be my first Sunday – and subsequently and in particular on the Ascension, on Whitsunday, and, unkindest fate, on Trinity, because, he wrote, 'We reckon you will be better at that than we are'. I agreed to this and you can imagine my feelings when, the Sunday before Whitsunday, my colleague (not Dr Miller), who was preaching that Sunday, began his sermon by saying, 'I don't know why, but I feel I've got to say something to you today on the Holy Spirit'. I said to myself, that makes two of us who don't know why you feel you've got to preach on the Holy Spirit when I've got to do so next Sunday. I asked him after the service if he knew what next Sunday was. He confessed his ignorance. 'Whitsunday, and I'm preaching.' He clutched his head in despair and penitence.

My ministerial friends at Montview accepted my criticism, and we discussed how the matter might be remedied. They thought of adopting a lectionary. They discussed the advisability of structured services based, in a flexible and sensible way, on the Christian Year. One of the ministerial team at that time was Dr Austin Lovelace, one of the most distinguished organists and choirmasters in America, and he gave wholehearted support for the idea of a structured service, saying that the music was left entirely to him, including the choice of hymns, which he felt was wrong and worked against the unity of the service. He had no idea what the lessons or the theme of the sermon was likely to be.

Since those far-off days there has been a much greater appreciation of the value of the ancient custom of observing the Christian Year, not only in America but in Scotland and in Africa and in many of what we call the Younger Churches. One of the contemporary tools to help busy ministers to shape their services is *The Worshipbook,* commissioned by three churches – the Cumberland Presbyterian Church, the Presbyterian Church in the United States, and the United Presbyterian Church in the USA. This was published in 1972 and is greatly admired and much used in services in other parts of the world. In 1993 a new and most impressive *Book of Common Worship* was authorised by the Presbyterian Church (USA) and the Cumberland Presbyterian Church, but, with few changes, the lectionaries of both volumes are the same as in *The Worshipbook*.

Of the chapters that follow on the general theme of preaching through the year, the first six will concentrate on the Christian Year itself, while the last three will be devoted to preaching on special days – holy communion, holy baptism, confirmation, marriage, In Memoriam services, ordination, and so on, as well as natural occasions, Harvest Thanksgiving, Thanksgiving, civic and community services, plus a concluding lecture on preaching and on the ministry in general.

I commend the observance of the Christian Year to you for your consideration for very practical reasons and out of my own experience. You are called to lead your people in worship Sunday by Sunday. Sunday by Sunday (and this usually means every Sunday, since most ministries in Scotland and America are sole ministries) you will be called to preach the word of God. It is an exciting, a humbling, and a frightening prospect.

After six months in my first parish I found that I was spending more and more time, longer and longer into the wee sma' hours of Sunday morning, not on putting into my poor words the word of God, but on finding what I was to preach on. Could I find a suitable passage? There were plenty of suitable passages. Could I find a text? The Bible was full of texts. What theme would I take, what doctrine would I expound, what heresies (that they had never thought of until I told them) would I expose? There were an embarrassing number of themes, a variety of doctrines, and in its long history the Church had thrown up a sufficient number of heresies to keep us going for long enough. But it didn't work out that way. I found that I was wasting an awful lot of time looking for a passage, a text, a theme, or a doctrine to preach on. I found that I was preaching on what suited my tastes, my interest, and not the needs of my people. I discovered that there were great gaps in my preaching, and that in no sense could what I was doing be described as proclaiming 'the whole counsel of God'. I realised that while I had worked on a syllabus and a scheme for the Sunday school and the Bible class and the Youth Fellowship, I was living from hand to mouth Sunday by Sunday. My people were getting no systematic teaching on the faith, and I knew that before very long there would be signs of serious spiritual malnutrition. In short, I was being selective in a totally subjective way, which was unsatisfying to my people and unsatisfactory to me. It took me more than two years to find an answer. This disciple required a discipline, and I found it and have continued to find it in what I have already described as a flexible and sensible use of a lectionary based on the Christian Year.

The use of a lectionary goes back to the synagogue, where there were proper lessons for special occasions, and where on ordinary sabbaths there was the practice of *lectio continua*, that is, reading through the books of the Old Testament. There is evidence from Justin Martyr that the early Church followed this practice by adding to the Old Testament selected lessons from the Gospels and appropriate pericopes or passages from the apostolic writings. *Lectio continua* has an almost unbroken history in the Church to this day, and I will have something to say later about this practice. I find contemporary Reformed support for my plea for the use of a lectionary in the index volume of Karl Barth's *Church Dogmatics*. The second part of this volume is headed 'Aids for the Preacher' and consists of commentaries on lessons for each Sunday of the year based on a German lectionary. It is edited by Dr Bromiley of Pasadena and Dr Torrance of Edinburgh. There is also support from the Roman Catholic Church in a book by Father Gerard Sloyan, *Commentary on the New Lectionary* (New York: Paulist Press, 1975), which has the same intention as the 'Aids for the Preacher'.

It is, I think, significant that all the great religions make use of regular occasions in the course of the year for special observances. It was a characteristic, as I have indicated, of the Jewish religion in which our Lord and the apostles and the early Christians were brought up. There was the Passover, for example, celebrating the deliverance from bondage in Egypt; and among the natural seasons there was Pentecost, the Feast of Weeks, and Tabernacles, which was the equivalent of our Harvest Thanksgiving. The most frequent and common of all such observances for the Jew was the fulfilling of the injunction to 'remember the sabbath day' (*ie* the seventh day, Saturday) and 'keep it holy'.

As early as the earliest part of the New Testament there is clear evidence of the Christian observance of Sunday. This may have begun as early as the week after Christ's resurrection, for according to John's Gospel it was a week after Easter that the disciples were assembled in the Upper Room and Jesus appeared (John 20:26). In the book of Acts (20:7ff) we already find the Christians gathering on the first day of the week for preaching and the breaking of bread. And in 1 Corinthians 16:2 you have the first mention of the Sunday collection. The day was known as the Lord's Day, and this became the germ of the Christian Calendar or Year.

This change from Saturday to Sunday as THE DAY of worship was not change for change's sake. It is an indication of how supremely important the Easter event was for the Christians and the Christian faith. Even the most casual reading of the book of Acts or the letters of Paul makes clear that the central note of the preaching of the early Church was that Christ both died and rose again. That he had to be born and live and teach before he died and rose is assumed as a shattering glimpse of the obvious, but it is on the central event, the death and resurrection of Jesus, that the gospel is founded. This is the very kernel of the *kerygma*. The Christian gospel is not a system of ideas, but the story of the saving acts of the Lord. It is right and natural that those great acts should not only be recorded in Scripture and summarised in the creeds, but that they should be lived over again, read about, thought about, proclaimed and interpreted year by year. They happened in time and in a divine sequence, and they should be recalled in sequence in time.

If one follows the evolution of the Christian Year it is obvious that it was not imposed on the Church by some liturgical lunatic but was a natural growth whose origin we see in Scripture in the development of Sunday as the Lord's Day. The annual observance of Easter clearly is connected with the observance of the Passover. Easter was the Feast of Feasts. It was for many centuries commonly known as the Passover or Pasch. 'Christ our passover is sacrificed for us. Therefore let us keep the feast' (I Corinthians 5:7-8, KJV). And to this day the date of Easter is determined by the Passover moon. It became very early a historical memorial of the actual events and a season of rejoicing. Thus you have the recapitulation of the week leading up to Easter which we commonly call Holy Week, and the recalling of the appearances after Easter. The post-Easter period as a time of celebration was determined by the fact of the coming of the Holy Spirit at the first Whitsunday, which coincided, as we all know, with another Jewish festival, the Feast of Weeks or Harvest, which fell, as the name Pentecost implies, on the fiftieth day after the Passover. The common people are reluctant to give up their ancient festivals, and Easter falling at Passovertide and the coming of the Spirit at Pentecost, with the events of the week leading up to Easter, provided the Church with the first period in which to recall and to rejoice in the death and the rising of Jesus Christ, which have always been the central facts of our faith, as evidenced not least by the amount of space given to those events in the four Gospels.

But the Easter season not only commemorated the death and resurrection of Jesus as historic events; they also provided an opportunity of interpreting those events, and more, they offered to the people the possibility of the Christian experience of entering into, of sharing in, and of applying the benefits of Christ's death and resurrection, of which the act of Christian baptism was the seal and the sign. As Paul wrote to the Romans (6:3-4):

> *Do you not know that all of us who have been baptised into Christ Jesus were baptised into his death? We were buried therefore with him by baptism into death, so that as Christ was raised from the dead by the glory of the Father, we too might walk in newness of life.*

So by the early third century the celebration of Easter had gained a baptismal character and was the principal occasion, especially in the Western Church, for the introduction and reception of new converts into the Christian community.

This led in the time before Easter to a long period of instruction, and it is to this that we probably owe the beginning of the pre-Easter period which is called Lent. The length of the period varied in different parts of the Church. In the West it appears to have been generally six weeks, which tended to become forty weekdays of fasting (Sunday not being a fast day) in commemoration of our Lord's temptation and forty days' fasting in the wilderness, and so you get the beginning of the fast falling on the Wednesday preceding the sixth Sunday before Easter, commonly called Ash Wednesday. This period was a time for consideration of themes like temptation, sin, repentance, and new life as God's gift to us in Christ confirmed in his death for our sins and his rising to new life.

The culmination of this period in the concentration on the week before Easter was strongly influenced by another fact. By the fourth century Jerusalem had become noted as a place of Christian pilgrimage and, as was natural, there were, as there still are, local observances of the events in our Lord's life at the traditional spots where those events occurred. I have a vivid memory of a visit to the well at Sychar. I remember drinking from the well, which is deep, and I have a photograph of my wife sitting by the well, and of walking up the street in Emmaus one enchanted evening and looking at the foundations of the little excavated houses and wondering, was it there, or there, or there that the words in wrought iron above the gateway to the convent at Emmaus were spoken, '*Domine, mane nobiscum*'?

There exists a description by a Spanish lady of a visit she paid to Jerusalem about the year 385. She tells of a procession of palms from Bethany to Olivet on the Sunday before Easter (Palm Sunday), of the celebration of the Lord's Supper on the Thursday, and the three hours spent on the Friday at the site of Calvary. Thus, the keeping of Holy Week began in a kind of historical way, following through the events as they happened.

So you have thus early the development of the beginnings of the Christian Year with what is called the Easter cycle. It was later stretched backwards – as far as I can see, more or less to fill a gap between the beginning of the Easter cycle and the end of the Christmas cycle – to the ninth Sunday before Easter, where you have those quaint-sounding days called Septuagesima, Sexagesima, and Quinquagesima – 70, 60, 50 days respectively before Easter – which is, I think, an understandable attempt to make the Christian Year coincide with the calendar year and fill every minute with sixty seconds' worth of distance run. But I myself have never observed or even mentioned Septuagesima, Sexagesima or Quinquagesima.

That brings me to the origin of the Christmas cycle, which is both biblical and historical.

It is a verifiable fact that the space in the New Testament devoted to the birth of Jesus is very small compared with the space devoted to his death and resurrection and the events leading up to them. Only two of the four Evangelists give any details of the birth of Jesus and the legendary accounts of events leading up to his coming. There is nothing in Mark, the earliest Gospel, and John's prologue is a massive and meaningful interpretation of his coming but with a minimum of detail. There is nothing about Jesus' birth in the book of Acts and precious little in Paul's writings or in the other writings in the New Testament.

It was later than the New Testament, though still very early in the life of the Church, that attention began to be paid to Christmas. It probably began with the heartfelt desire of the early Christians to celebrate the birth and the birthday of their Lord. The date of his birth was not known. There is nothing strange about that. We don't know the birthday of John Knox, or for that matter, coming to our own period, of Jomo Kenyatta. The need was felt to celebrate Jesus' birthday, and in the West the imaginative date chosen was December 25, which was the end of the winter solstice, the beginning of the coming of the light. In the East they chose January 6, again to mark the coming of the light, the showing, the manifestation, the Epiphany. Eventually West and East accepted each other's festivals, and so you have the celebration of Christmas on December 25 and extending to the twelve days of Christmas and then going on to the celebration of Epiphany, in which we think of the worldwide, universal significance of the coming of Jesus Christ as the Light of the World. This is the proper period for considering the implications for the Church of mission, and the obligations of the Church to mission, beginning at Jerusalem and stretching out to the ends of the earth. It should be noted that there is an inbuilt flexibility from year to year at this point of Epiphany. Epiphany can be as little as four Sundays or as many as nine, depending on how early or how late Easter falls. There is plenty of biblical material, as we shall see when we come to consider what we are to preach through the year.

Historically the observance of and the thinking about the birth of Jesus was greatly influenced by the theological controversies regarding the person of Christ which dominated the theological thinking and the early councils of the Church in the fourth and fifth centuries, and which were marked by the findings of the Council of Nicaea in 325 and by the Council of Chalcedon over a century later in 451. This is still a contemporary concern and still being discussed and controverted by subsequent publications. I will discuss what I have to say about the birth of Jesus in the course of the book. It was, it should be

I now quote two passages from the preface to the great *Prayer Book* of Edward VI which I think is primarily Episcopal with its emphasis on order and uniformity, but with provision for diversity:

Whereas heretofore there have been great diversity in saying and singing in Churches within this realm: some following Salisbury use, some Hereford use, and some the use of Bangor, some of York, some of Lincoln; now from henceforth all the whole realm shall have but one use. And forasmuch as nothing can be so plainly set forth but doubts may arise in the use and practice of the same; to appease all such diversity (if any arise) ... the parties that so doubt, or diversely take anything, shall always resort to the Bishop of the Diocese, who by his discretion shall take order for the quieting and appeasing of the same ... and if the Bishop of the Diocese be in doubt, then he may send for the regulation thereof to the Archbishop.

It is interesting to note that the preface also contains this statement:

In these our doings we condemn no other nations nor prescribe anything but to our own people only: for we think it convenient that every country should use such ceremonies as they shall think best to the setting forth of God's honour and glory.

If Charles I and Charles II and Archbishop Laud had read and heeded that part of the preface from the revised *Prayer Book* of Edward VI we might have been spared the bloody Covenanting period in Scotland.

I quote from the preface to your own church's *Worshipbook* (1972). There it is written: 'The *Worshipbook* is a Presbyterian book. It is faithful to that tradition. The *Worshipbook* is an ecumenical book. It attempts to adopt ... the best that fellow Christians in other Churches and traditions have to offer.'

Presbyterians value freedom and variety in worship, but they noted, always for a catechetical purpose, to give sound and systematic teaching, that the people might know who and what most surely was believed, that the observance of the Christian Year revolved around the three facts of Christ's coming, and of his dying, and of his rising to share the life of his Spirit with us. This was the clear purpose of both the Easter and the Christmas cycles.

By analogy with the Easter cycle it was thought fitting to extend the Christmas cycle to have a period of preparation for Christmas: this period is called Advent. It is found well established by the seventh century, though here again the period is not universally the same. In some places it goes back to the middle of November. In Milan they still keep five weeks, but at Rome and in the West generally four weeks before Christmas were regarded as a sufficient period of preparation by the Church. The secular and commercial world can hardly wait for the beginning of November before it begins to tell us that Christmas is coming. They have their own reasons, but I think there is something to be said – and I will say it – for not suddenly, without any preparation, inviting each other to 'Hark the herald angels sing'. The absence of such a period of preparation may result in an unbiblical and romantic concentration on the child in the manger rather than on the coming of the Christ, the Saviour of the world.

Chronologically we see that between the Easter cycle and the Christmas cycle there is a gap of about half a year after Pentecost. In the larger part of Christendom those Sundays are dated 'after Pentecost'. In the West, and logically, the first Sunday after Pentecost came to be observed as a festival in honour of the Holy Trinity, and the Sundays thereafter up to Advent were dated 'after Trinity'. The *Book of Common Worship* follows the older 'after Pentecost' dating, but marks the first Sunday after Pentecost, in brackets, 'Trinity Sunday'. While I am in favour of the preacher on occasion embarking on the deep waters of the doctrine of the Trinity, there is more to be said than mere antiquity in favour of the older tradition. The structure of the Christian Year is governed very properly by events, by God's mighty acts, by incarnation and resurrection and the coming of the Holy Spirit; whereas Trinity is the commemoration not so much of an event as of a doctrine.

The post-Pentecost half-year has been used traditionally and very properly as a time when the Church looks at the early Church and what the Spirit-filled community began to do and to teach as reflected in the Acts and the epistles, and to hear what God's Spirit is saying to us today. Such a custom, under the guidance as always of the Holy Spirit, provides more than half the year when there is ample scope for that liberty which the minister ought to have in the choice of theme, and provides us opportunity for preaching through one of the books of the Bible, or preaching a series on Spirit-filled men and women of the Bible, or a series on the Old Testament prophets, or the letters to the seven churches in the book of Revelation, or on what, more directly, the Spirit is saying to the congregation or to the Church at large today.

Throughout the Christian Year there is and there must be freedom for the preacher to respond as the Spirit moves, to fill in the framework or to adjust the framework, which is by no means inflexible; and for half the year there is no restriction at all, though the discipline of a lectionary is not to be despised and, indeed, is a very present help in times, which come to us all, when we are troubled about what to preach and are convinced that we have preached ourselves out.

In the rest of this chapter I want to look with you at what happened to the observance of the Christian Year prior to the Reformation and after the Reformation.

In the Dark Ages, when the Church suffered a decline almost throughout Christendom, there is evidence that the observance of the Christian Year fell into desuetude. The framework had collapsed through neglect, and one consequence was the introduction of meaningless ceremonies, the multiplication of saints' days, and the paganisation of the great festivals which remained. The Scriptures, when they were read, which was infrequently, were of course read in Latin, and it was only in the decade or so before the Reformation that the Church issued catechisms in the vernacular, sometimes with the injunction that the clergy to whom they were distributed had to lend them only sparingly to the laity. The clerics who neglected to study the catechism were to be fined, and they were enjoined not only to read selected portions on Sunday in church, but to prepare themselves by constant daily reading, 'lest' – and I quote – 'they expose themselves to the ridicule of the hearers when, through want of preparation they stammer and stumble in mid-course of reading'. Preaching, of course, was rare; the Provincial Councils of the Church in Scotland prior to the Reformation make it clear that this was so when, for example, they enjoin rectors and bishops to preach personally four times a year, or – if unable to do so – to study until they are. I have used evidence from Roman Catholic sources because in a polemical age it was difficult to be fair in criticism. It is possible, but it is not necessary, to accept George Buchanan's story that many priests condemned the New Testament as a dangerous work written by Martin Luther. But it is worth noting that Sir David Lindsay, who never became a Protestant, in his great pre-Reformation play *A Satire of the Three Estates*, makes Spiritualitie (the clergy) reply to the question as to whether he has ever read the New Testament, by saying:

> *Na, Sir, by him that our Lord Jesus sould*
> *I read never the New Testament, nor Auld,*
> *Nor ever think to do, Sir, be the Rude*
> *I heir freiris say, that reiding dois na gude.*

There were those in the Roman Catholic Church who deplored this state of affairs and tried to remedy it, but clearly there was opposition, and the Reformers had a long way to go before they could recover the practice of the Fathers and repair the framework and recover the supremacy of the Bible as containing the Word of God. They only slowly and in part achieved the first, and while the new translations of the Bible into the vernacular throughout Europe made a breakthrough possible to the hearers of the Word, the regular use of a lectionary came later. The very degradation of the Christian Year and its cluttering with all kinds of fanciful ceremonial and saints' days in part explain the slowness of some of the Reformers in preparing a satisfactory *Book of Common Order*. It is not historically accurate to say that the Reformers had no liturgy. The first edition of Knox's *Book of Common Order* contains instructions on how to find the date of Easter, for example, on which, as I have indicated, the framework of the Christian Year depends. Luther and Calvin both produced liturgies, as did most of the Reformers. And before 1560 Knox used the *English Prayer Book* both in England and when he ministered at Frankfurt. He influenced the inclusion of the 'black rubric' in the revised Prayer Book of 1552, which declares that by kneeling at communion 'no adoration is intended or ought to be done'. Indeed, for some years in Scotland Edward VI's *Prayer Book* of 1549 continued in use alongside the *Book of Common Order*.

If in the background to the work of the Reformers there was a decay of the worship of the Church and a secularisation of its great festivals, which explains some of the 'cleansing' that took place and even the prohibition against keeping Christmas and Easter, it is also clear from cases brought before presbyteries that in many places minister and people did observe those festivals for many years after the Reformation in Scotland. In England, in part, the position of the pre-Reformation Church may not have been quite so lamentable as it was in Scotland, and therefore the cleansing was not quite so drastic. There are two other factors to be borne in mind which explain the emergence of the *English Prayer Book* in England while nothing comparable appeared in Scotland. First, the English Reformation was much more Lutheran in character compared with the Calvin-influenced Scottish Reformation. Luther was more interested in worship than Knox. Second, the Reformation in England had the support of the king, and therefore it was less radically political than it was in Scotland, where the queen and many of the leading nobles were Catholic. That meant the Scottish Reformers had a harder and a more distracting struggle and therefore tended to be much more suspicious of anything in the heritage of the old Church and more sweeping in the changes that they made. This to some extent explains the absence in Scotland of anything comparable to the *English Prayer Book*. The great work to be done was the proclaiming of the Word. That was where the accent lay. As Professor John Leith points out in his Introduction to the *Reformed Tradition* (Atlanta: John Knox Press, 1977), it has been argued that, in Calvin's liturgy of 1545, the sermon was the only form in which Scripture was read in the liturgy. It has been contended that the sermon was the Word of God in the service, and the Second Helvetic Confession specifically refers to the sermon as the Word of God. That is not the stance of the Scots Confession in which Knox had a hand. That – one of the great confessions – while exalting the preaching of the Word as one of the notes of the true Kirk, makes it clear that the Word of God is contained in the books of the Old and New Testaments. I don't think either Calvin or Knox was very interested in liturgy. The Calvin liturgy is not original but is derived from one which in turn is a reformation of the Mass by Schwartz at Strasbourg and later revised by, among others, Martin Bucer.

There was, therefore, particularly in Scotland, something of a gap in the ordering of worship, and, as elsewhere in a period of reformation and change, considerable variety and no uniformity in orders of worship, despite the existence of a Scottish *Book of Common Order*. This in part explains Laud's vain attempt to impose his Prayer Book on the Church in Scotland in the seventeenth century, though it does not excuse the rudeness of the attempt. It has been made clear that it was not a Prayer Book that was being objected to, but Laud's Prayer Book, but that is a little specious. The Scottish *Book of Common Order* was and continued to be not comparable in its range with any of the English Prayer Books.

One of the main influences on worship from the seventeenth century onwards, in Scotland and in America, was the Puritan Revolution and the work of the Westminster Assembly of 1643. It is from this period that we have the emphatic prohibition of any other days than the Lord's Day as Holy Days, and a discouragement of the great festivals: hence the dismantling of the framework of the Christian Year in England and its discouragement in Scotland. The Puritans disliked the Establishment. The *Prayer Book* was part of the Establishment, therefore it must be bad – therefore it must go. They maintained that it had undercut the significance of preaching – and there was some truth in that. In Scotland – though the Westminster Directory never had the force that the Westminster Confession had in the life of the Kirk – the people had good reason to be suspicious of attempts at imposing an *English Prayer Book*. In America, English Presbyterians, Puritans, and Scots Presbyterians brought with them the practices of their homeland, and in some respects clung to them the more fiercely because they were from home and because they gave a freedom which was appropriate to a new land.

One other influence on the development of worship in America parallels the Scottish experience of the attempt to impose episcopacy from which stems a quite irrational fear of bishops and a distaste for anything Anglican. I refer to the fact that in the American Revolution the Episcopal Church in America expressed its ingrained Erastianism by siding with the imperial power. This may have caused the slowing up of appreciation of what is worthwhile in the observance of the Christian Year and the sensible use of a lectionary. From this position Scotland and America are recovering, and learning from one another and, I hope, rediscovering what the practice of the Church was for over a thousand years. I will be content if I can make a small contribution to this recovery, to the good of the Church and to assist those of you who are going to be part of its ministry into the twenty-first century to preach the Word of God and the glorious gospel of our Lord and Saviour, Jesus Christ, in all its fullness.

Any plea for increased observance of the Christian Year must always try to hold in balance two apparently contradictory aims. On the one hand there is the aim of having an ordered scheme of teaching and of preaching, biblically based, which will inform and inspire our people in the knowledge and love of God, Father, Son, and Holy Spirit. There is also something to be said for the Church, locally, nationally, and universally, thinking together as much as possible about the mighty saving acts of God, as we do in fact at Christmas and Easter. On the other hand our Lord has promised to guide his Church through the Holy Spirit, and the wind bloweth where it listeth, and there must be freedom for the Spirit to do just that.

The Church and the churches have not always succeeded in this difficult matter of holding in balance order and freedom. Is this another aspect of the difficulty of reconciling law and grace? Understandably, churches with an Episcopal polity have tended to emphasise order at the expense of freedom, while churches with a conciliar and congregational polity have erred in the other direction in emphasising freedom at the expense of order.

It is an interesting exercise to read that neglected part of books of common order, prayer books, worship books – whatever you care to call them – namely, the prefaces. Almost without exception they make a point in one way or another of emphasising this matter of a balance between order and freedom.

I quote from the preface to the Church of Scotland's *Book of Common Order* (1940):

> *Liberty in the conduct of worship is a possession which the Church of Scotland will not surrender. But a Service Book is necessary to express the mind of the Church with regard to its offices of worship in orders and forms which, while not fettering individual judgment in particular, will set the norm.*

Very Presbyterian with its priority given to liberty! A similar but shorter note occurs in the latest *Book of Common Order* (1994).

emphasise equally the virtue of orderliness. It is hardly necessary to state that the book is for voluntary use. Leaders in worship will supply their own variations. To do so will be to please, not disappoint, those who have prepared the book ...

As is known, Presbyterians are not required to follow a lectionary as they plan for worship on the Lord's Day. On the other hand, the following of a lectionary, with flexibility, helps assure a congregation that it will not, in the course of a period of years, neglect the great teachings of the Bible.

In 1993 a new *Book of Common Worship* was published in America for the United Presbyterian Church. This is not only one of the best books of Common Worship in English published by any Reformed Church, it also has a masterly preface of 13 pages in which it outlines the history of common worship. I quote the opening sentence of the preface. It reads: 'Worship is at the very heart of the Church's life.' And one more sentence at the top of page 9 of the preface: 'This book honours the blend of the Church, of freedom within form, that characterises Presbyterian Worship'.

The same note is shown in the preface to the 1994 Church of Scotland *Book of Common Order*.

The words are theirs, but here again I would say most heartily: 'Them's my sentiments.'

1

ADVENT
AND CHRISTMAS

I CONCLUDED the Introduction with a quotation from the preface to *The Worshipbook*. Let me begin this chapter with a rather more lengthy quotation from the preface to the Westminster Directory for the Public Worship of God which was part of the work of the Westminster Assembly which concluded its labours in 1643. Of the Directory, which they produced in addition to the Westminster Confession of Faith, the authors have this to say:

Our care hath been to hold forth such things as are of divine institution in every ordinance; and other things we have endeavoured to set forth according to the rules of Christian prudence, agreeing to the general rules of the word of God; our reasoning therein being only, that the general heads, the sense and scope of the prayers and other parts of public worship, being known to all, there may be a consent of all the churches in those things that contain the substance of the service and worship of God; and the ministers may be hereby directed, in their administrations, to keep like soundness in doctrine and prayer, and may, if need be, have some help and furniture, and yet so as they become not hereby slothful and negligent in stirring up the gifts of Christ in them; but that each one, by meditation, by taking heed to himself, and the flock of God committed to him, and by wise observing the ways of divine providence, may be careful to furnish his heart and tongue with further or other materials of prayer and exhortation, as shall be needful on all occasions.

Two or three points would appear from this passage. First,

that in addition to ordinances 'of divine institution' they are setting forth 'other things ... according to the rules of Christian prudence', or, as we might say, what seems wise and sensible. Second, that in doing so they intend to give only 'general heads', and notice the two reasons they mention for doing so: that 'there may be a consent of all the churches in those things that contain the substance of the service ... and [that] the ministers may be ... directed, in their administrations, to keep like soundness in doctrine [and have] some help and furniture, and yet so as they become not ... slothful and negligent'. In other words, they were trying to keep a balance between a unity of pattern and thought throughout the Church in its worship while at the same time avoiding a dull uniformity and the danger of encouraging laziness or inhibiting the exercise of individual gifts which under the guidance of the Holy Spirit may, to use the words with which the quotation ends, 'furnish ... heart and tongue with further or other materials of prayer and exhortation, as shall be needful upon all occasions'.

In commending the practice of following the Christian Year on the grounds that this would insure that the great biblical events and the doctrines arising from those events will be covered in an orderly way, I have not emphasised what is given in the quotation as one of the reasons for their Directory, namely 'that there may be a consent of all the churches in those things that contain the substance of the service'. No doubt historically they had in mind a consent not only of the Presbyterian Church in England, but also the hoped-for unity of that Church with the Church of Scotland. I would plead for consideration to be given not so much for uniformity of worship but for unity in the thinking of the Church and the churches which would, I believe, be helped by all of us working within the framework of the Christian Year. This, of course, is happening increasingly, and increasingly this expresses and witnesses to a unity among the churches in the things most surely believed, which amid much diversity leads to that true unity in Christ for which our Lord prayed. There is much to be said for the concerted impact of the thinking and praying of Christians of one heart and one mind, of the same or different denominations, at one and the same time, in all the world for all the world, and all with the evangelical aim that the world may believe.

It is my intention to be mindful of the caveat in the Directory that, while I am giving you 'some help and furniture', what I do in that respect should not encourage laziness or carelessness, nor should it provide you with substitutes for thinking out your own sermons or series of sermons. I am, therefore, proposing in each chapter to look in general at what are the great themes which ought to be dominant in the different seasons of the year, and then to go on briefly to suggest in the barest outline how those themes might be approached and expanded. I begin with Advent, leading up to Christmas and the Sundays immediately following Christmas.

What is the main theme of Advent? Why Christmas? In part we have to go back to the Old Testament to find the essential necessity for the incarnation. When you look at the Old Testament passages prescribed in the lectionary for the Sundays in Advent, you will find that in one way or another they all speak of a promise of God that, somehow or other, will be fulfilled by his coming, his advent. Apart from particular selected passages, we find that, while the Old Testament witnesses to the reality that we call God, behind this world, the world both of creation and of ongoing history, we cannot fail to notice that there is also and intertwined with the faith a very considerable degree of agnosticism. God is Yea and Amen, a positive statement and a giver of statements about himself and the world and history. 'Thus saith the Lord' is the predominant and the characteristic prefatory note of the Old Testament.

But alongside that there is also a frank agnosticism. You find it in the prophets: 'Verily thou art a God that hidest thyself, O God of Israel, the Saviour' (Isaiah 45:15, KJV). And the literature which most clearly reflects the human experience of God, the book of Job for example, and many of the Psalms, again and again ponder the impenetrable mystery of God. 'Oh that I knew where I might find him!' says Job (23:3, KJV). And after a long passage declaiming the wonders of the world, he says in awe (26:14, KJV), 'Lo, these are parts of his ways: but how little a portion is heard of him? but the thunder of his power who can understand?' The Psalms are at one and the same time evidence of patient faith and of impatience and distress because of an awareness of God's absence. 'O satisfy us early with thy mercy' (Psalm 90:14, KJV). 'How long, O LORD, how long?' (Psalm 13:1, KJV). Our Lord's cry from the cross is a quotation from Psalm 22: 'My God, my God, why hast thou forsaken me?' (Psalm 22:1; see Matthew 27:46, Mark 15:34).

And this is not something peculiar to the Old Testament. Paul at Athens found the Greeks had made an altar to a god incognito. And it is Paul who says: 'How unsearchable are his judgments, and his ways past finding out!' (Romans 11:33, KJV). There is a sense in which God is always the unknown God. We can never get his measure. We can never master God. God is always the Lord.

But the Old Testament – faced with the inscrutability of God and our inability, unaided, to search out God – prophesied, foretold, that God himself, some time, somehow, would come to show us what he is like. Of his pure grace he would reveal himself. In a sense the very fact of his revelation is our salvation. Something of that is what you find hinted at, often obscurely but with a certain confidence, in the Old Testament. The one who is to come at that advent is known by many names and pictured as appearing in different forms, but the Messiah, the anointed and appointed one, will come to this world and to our need. That is the necessity of CHRISTMAS.

The good news is that God was in Christ. The first Christian confession on which the Church is founded is Peter's word: 'Thou art the Christ, the Son of the living God' (Matthew 16:16, KJV). One of the reasons why Advent from the earliest days of the

Church was also connected with baptism, is that it was at our Lord's baptism that the word of God and the witness of God is heard. 'This is my beloved Son' (Matthew 3:17, KJV).

It is also possibly connected with baptism because that sacrament is the expression of the perpetual coming of God in Christ, of his pure grace, to all. Christmas not only recalls that 'a little child the Saviour came', but it proclaims the faith that is implicit in infant baptism that the Saviour comes to a little child. If you have the opportunity of celebrating infant baptism during Advent, the connection between Christmas and baptism is relevant and should be expounded to your congregation.

You should also take the opportunity Advent provides of teaching your people something about the Bible and in particular about the relationship between the Old Testament and the New Testament. In Scotland, the second Sunday in Advent is often called Bible Sunday, and, as the name suggests, is devoted to giving thanks for Holy Scripture, while at the same time pointing out that we do not worship a book, even one which contains the Word of God, because the Word became flesh, and it is him alone we worship. He is the object of our faith and our hope and our love. It is also used, Bible Sunday, to commend the work of the Bible societies and the labours of Bible translators – to whom we are all indebted, not least in our own day. In recent years there has been a great increase in the number of contemporary translations into English which has led to an increase, I believe, in Bible reading. We have an added responsibility for that reason to teach people how to read the Bible, and Advent on at least one Sunday provides one opportunity of doing so, and it would be possible to devote all the Advent Sundays to the Bible. What it is. How it came to be. Is it true? What do we mean by saying that it is true? Why did the Word become flesh? And what does that mean? There is another theme that is properly dealt with at Advent. It is a difficult theme – almost as difficult as the suggested series on the Bible. I refer to what is called the second coming. The lectionary points to this theme in proposing lessons from the Bible which speak not of the first Advent but of the last Advent: *eg* 2 Peter 3:8-14; 1 Thessalonians 5:1-6; and apocalyptic passages from the Gospels, *eg* Matthew 24:36-44 and Luke 21:25-36.

Difficult? Yes, but it has to be tackled some time, not just because it is there in the Bible, and not just because some people make more of the second coming than the Bible does and thereby are classified as eccentric, even though we are to blame because we commonly err by making too little of this theme. Historically, again and again, heresies and distortions of the faith have arisen, in part because the Church has failed to give a proper place to some biblical truth; and the heretics often do the Church a service by pointing us back to the truth which, by magnifying, they distort. But it has to be tackled, because one of the commonest questions today is: 'What is the world coming to?' The answer is the second Advent, which is at one and the same time a cautionary answer and a comfortable answer. Cautionary in the sense of the word: 'For judgment am I come' (John 10:39, KJV). Comfortable in the sense that as in the beginning so in its ending the world is in the control of the God whom we have seen in the coming of Jesus Christ. In a time which is uncomfortably aware that the picture of the end of the world in Peter and Hebrews and the Gospels could be a realistic and contemporary picture, we have a duty to point out the hope in the connection between the first Advent and the last Advent.

On this matter of relevance may I say this: there is sometimes a fear expressed that a rigid observance of the Christian Year in your preaching may lead to a cold irrelevance to the day-to-day needs of your people. You may, in the old Quaker phrase, be failing 'to speak to their condition'. I have already emphasised that lectionaries and calendars are there as a guide, and that they should never be used inflexibly or allowed to quench the spirit. But let me add two things from my experience: the first is that I have been again and again surprised precisely at how pointedly some theme or some passage of Scripture from the Christian Year and the lectionary fitted in with what I felt the Spirit was saying to me to say to my people. And this is not my subjective experience alone. Again and again people in my congregation have told me that some word from the lessons prescribed for the day or the theme for the day spoke to them and to their condition.

The second observation I would make is this. It is a useful protection against the critic in the pew who will suspect and possibly accuse you of getting at him or her when you preach on the second coming or the virgin birth, for example, if you can point out that what you had to say you said because it arose naturally from the theme or lesson for the day. It is my experience that the observance of the Christian Year gives one an opportunity in a perfectly natural and relevant way of dealing with sometimes sensitive subjects, and that coming to such subjects in that way is more acceptable to a congregation than any apparently haphazard or subjective approach.

If the opportunity given by the Sundays in Advent preceding Christmas is properly used, the Church is prepared to celebrate the great fact of the incarnation at a much deeper level than would otherwise be the case. Without such a preparation there is a very real danger that Christmas will be romanticised, and the birth stories in the Gospels will be trivialised and emptied of deep meaning, and it will all, and only, be about a baby born in a stable and cradled in a manger. It is understandable that Christmas should be regarded as a children's festival, but we must be careful that it is not just dismissed as 'kids' stuff'. The proper preparation and leading up to Christmas through the Sundays preceding should leave your congregation in no doubt of the personal and cosmic significance of Christmas, and should help the faithful to come and adore him, Christ the Lord.

And not just the faithful. The early Reformers in Scotland discouraged the keeping of Christmas on pain of censure by the Church courts. They had their reasons: the festival had become secularised and was the occasion of alcoholically-induced joy. If you empty the festivals of their true joy you will get counterfeit joy. But the old records of Church courts indicate that the prohibition of the sacred festivals was no more successful than some other prohibition efforts. During the last fifty years I have noted the growing observance of Christmas and pondered the significance of the fact, for example, that one of the services which attracts the most extraordinary, the largest, and the most diverse congregation in the year is the Christmas Eve service. People come to that service, especially young people, who seldom if ever come to any other. People of all classes and races come to that service. People of all creeds and none – in Nairobi, for example – come to that service. Men and women in evening dress from parties in their homes or hotels, groups of young people in jeans, middle-class Africans, young lawyers and politicians, khaki-clad Africans, sometimes in tattered shorts and shirts – all would be there. Men from India and their wives in their colourful saris would be there. It was a moving sight to see this so varied a representation of humanity pouring up the steps to the church half an hour before midnight on Christmas Eve, and I have no doubt that it was and is due to a wistful feeling after the truth that in the coming of the Christ child there are good tidings of great joy for all people.

During the Second World War, I was a minister on Clydeside. One Christmas Eve I persuaded my kirk session that we ought to present a nativity play at Christmas which would consist of readings from Scripture, illustrated by tableaux on stage and by appropriate carols sung by the choir off stage, and that this should be presented at 11:30 pm and should end with the congregation singing 'O Come, All Ye Faithful'. They agreed, but privately thought that no one would come out in the blackout at that time of night. Three months' preparation went into that service. Young and old were involved. The Blackburn Aircraft Company made the Angel Gabriel's wings. A famous Clyde shipyard built the stage, and a silk and cotton manufacturer with a large Eastern trade gave cloth for the making of the costumes. The church sat a thousand people. By ten minutes past eleven there were 1200 people in church and the chief elder on the door came round in a panic saying, 'What are we to do, there are hundreds clamouring to get in?' We put those who didn't go home disappointed, into the main hall, where they were served with tea, and we repeated the service for another 600 people at 12:30 am. Why did they come? Was it because so many people in the community were involved? In part yes – and there is a lesson in that – but was it not because they were aware and dimly discerned the mystery of God come down to be with us sinful and sinning men and women, emptying himself and making himself of no reputation for love of the world, the Light of the World which shines in the darkness and which is never mastered?

We must neither overestimate nor underestimate the significance of this growing observance of Christmas. It has its dangers – the danger of sentimentality and romanticism. My contention is that we need have no fear of the focus of Christmas on the child in the manger if we have done our work in Advent to help our people to see and to know that the baby lying wrapped in swaddling clothes in a manger is Christ the Lord.

I am myself in favour of making the service on Christmas Day a short family service of carols, with the lesson the prologue to John's Gospel or the Christmas story in Luke. The sermon should be a brief Christmas greeting, followed, if possible, by an informal celebration of holy communion. This should be done if only to emphasise that there is an inescapable relationship between the cradle and the cross and the resurrection, and that though Christmas is a once-and-for-all event, he who came at the first Christmas is with us always to nourish and sustain us by his grace. It is a once-for-all-time event.

There is no great problem about what to preach about on the one or two Sundays after Christmas. It is not only a period which may include the last Sunday of the Old Year and the first Sunday of a New Year – and you may have something timely to say to the congregation about the turn of the natural year on one or the other of those Sundays (but I would suggest not both in the same period). Those Sundays are also devoted to the post-birth and boyhood incidents reported in the Gospels. And it is certainly possible to combine a reference to the natural year and the passing of time with, for example, the story of Simeon and Anna waiting for the coming of Christ in patient expectation.

One thing you will discover is that after the great festivals of Christmas and Easter there is a tendency for a drop in the spiritual temperature. This is expressed in some calendars by calling the Sunday after Easter, Low Sunday. This sense of being brought low may be accentuated on the Sunday after Christmas by the fact of another year's passing. And it is psychologically understandable. You should be sensitive to this, and the sensitivity should be expressed in your preaching on the Sunday after the great festivals. At such times one may recall the sobering word of James: 'What is your life? It is even a vapour, that appeareth for a little time, and then vanisheth away' (James 4:14, KJV). Or you could recall the splendidly simple, comfortable witness of the psalmist when he says: 'I was brought low, and he helped me' (Psalm 116:6, KJV).

One thing you should not do is, like some of the Christmas cards and some Christmas carols, prematurely bring the Wise Men onto the stage, except of course under the dramatic license given to you in a nativity play. The story of the Wise Men is too good and too significant a part of the gospel to get mixed up with the Lukan narrative. Biblically it is recorded as taking place vaguely after Jesus was born: the Magi came to a house not to a stable. It is permissible to ponder the contrast between the coming of the shepherds and the coming of the Wise Men, but that should be done as an introduction to Epiphany, which is the part of the Christian Year treated in the next chapter.

It is my intention in the second part of each chapter to suggest a brief outline series of sermon topics appropriate to the part of the Christian Year which we have been considering. It is not my intention to spoonfeed you, but rather to indicate some raw materials which are there for you yourselves to consider, perhaps to gather but certainly to prepare and to arrange – to cook and serve, not just according to your taste, but also according to the taste and needs of your congregation. I would advise you not just against preaching other people's sermons, but I would counsel you even against reading other people's sermons. It is not that you will be found out, which can happen, as it did posthumously to Peter Marshall. I was told in Washington not long after he died, that three or four sermons about to be published in a book of his had to be withdrawn because they were recognised as just too derivative and dependent on, among others, sermons of Professor James S. Stewart. The story is told in Scotland about 'J. S.' that once, on a holiday, he heard a minister preach one of his sermons almost verbatim. After the service he asked the minister how long he had taken over that sermon.

'Oh,' was the reply, 'about three hours.'

'Well,' said J. S., that prince of preachers and kindliest of men, 'it took me three days.'

But there are other and better reasons for cautioning you against reading other people's sermons. For one thing, I find when I have read a good sermon on a text or a passage, an incident or a parable, I can never preach on that text or passage simply because I find it difficult to convince myself that what I might have to say on the subject has not already been said, and said better than I could say it. More seriously, the fact is that, as the great Boston preacher Phillips Brooks said in the early years of this century in his book on preaching, preaching is truth through personality. The truth that we have to proclaim is eternal, given and unchanging. The person and the personality are unique and temporal. So are the personalities of the people with whom we are communicating. They have an influence on the form and style which shapes the content of the message. You must have regard to your audience.

One further suggestion: your direct reading for a particular sermon, the study of text and context, the comparative use of different translations and commentaries, should not take up too much of your preparation time. It should always be done, but 'twere well it were done quickly'. Normally, not more than a quarter of your reading should be devoted to reading with direct relevance to a particular sermon. Three-quarters of your reading should be general theological, New Testament and Old Testament study, the history of doctrine, and wider reading in literature, especially history and biography. Above all you must make and give time to waiting upon God lest you be found, having laboured much, to be speaking with authorities but not with the authority of one who has obeyed the injunction to hear what God the Lord will speak.

Now let me outline for you four possible Advent series.

I   The general heading for the first series would be Advent Questions, and they are all questions from the New Testament.

A   'What will be the sign of your coming?' (Matthew 24:3)
- The question the disciples asked Jesus as they looked at their civilisation, literally at Jerusalem and its fine buildings.
- Look at our civilisation in admiration and in criticism and learn from Jesus' warning.
- What then? Preach the gospel of the kingdom which his coming heralded.

B   John the Baptist's question addressed to Jesus: 'Are you he who is to come, or shall we look for another?' (Matthew 11:3)
- Any sermon on this question would have to say something not only about the Old Testament expectation, but about the healthy contemporary agnosticism that cannot accept that by searching we will find out God for our-

selves. In other words, it should deal with the necessity for revelation.

- It should also pay tribute to John the Baptist's part in the preparation for the coming of Christ and the dogged persistence implicit in the second part of the question: 'Shall we look for another?' Shall we? Where will we find another to save us from ourselves and to show us God? 'To whom can we go?'

C The last two questions are questions Jesus put to his disciples, and they are both from the same passage. The third question in the series – and the first of the two – is: 'Who do men say that the Son of man is?' (Matthew 16:13)

- Here you would have to say something, but not too much, about the title 'Son of man', and you would have to give it some contemporary as well as historical significance. People still toss this question around, and they give their various answers. You should evaluate and align with answers given today the reported answer in the text: John the Baptist (popular), Elijah (intended compliment), one of the prophets (kindly dismissive).

D The fourth question, and the second persistent and personal question of Jesus: 'But who do *you* say I am?' (Matthew 16:15, my emphasis)

- The necessity for personal decision. The temptation to let other people determine our indetermination.
- The persistence of Jesus. The significance of the answer of Peter.
- The significance of the response of Jesus to that answer of Peter's followed by Peter's contradiction and Jesus' recognition of the devil in Peter, and in us all, no matter how strong our commitment. But it is on such rocky material that Jesus builds his Church.

II The second series might be given the general title of Preparing for Christmas. Here you might begin with a sermon on:

A The world to which Christ came. This would be a sermon on the text of Galatians 4:4.
• Find out in what sense the time was ripe.
• Draw a picture of the Mediterranean world.
• Are there parallels and similarities with our world today? Christmas is coming. Are you ready for Christmas?

B The second sermon might home in on Israel, for Christ didn't just come to the world in general but to Israel in particular, and if you want a title for this second sermon it might be 'The Home State to Which Christ Came'. And here you would look at the Bible and the preparation for Christ's coming in the Old Testament and bring the story up to date with the beginning of the New Testament. You might find your text in Luke 1:16-17: 'A people prepared [for the Lord].'

C The third sermon should pan in closer still, to the family circumstances and the visit of Mary to Elizabeth. The title of this sermon might be 'The Preparation in the Home'. Christmas is a family festival. The coming of Jesus was a family concern from the beginning. Expand on the relationship between Elizabeth and Mary. It would be in order to make a reference to the virgin birth, if only to point out that like most births this was also a family affair. Mary stayed with Elizabeth three months. Perhaps your text could be Luke 1:56.

D The fourth sermon would be on the preparation in the heart.

The hert aye's the pairt aye
That maks us richt or wrang.

- And perhaps as a text you might take 'Mary kept all these things and pondered them in her heart' (Luke 2:19, KJV); or alternatively you might consider the favourable reference to Elizabeth and Zechariah in Luke 1:6.
- Christmas is not only the hope of the bad, it is also the fulfilment of the hope and patience of the good. There is, in addition to Zechariah and Elizabeth, the old couple, Simeon and Anna.

III A title for a third series might be Four Advents, and the first sermon might be on:

A The Eternal Advent, and the text would be the difficult but great word, 'Before Abraham was, I am' (John 8:58). The point you have to get across is that Jesus Christ is not a new God but the old, eternal God who has always been at work from the very beginning. 'In the beginning God ...'. You would indicate that that is what John is saying in his prologue. 'In the beginning was the Word .... And the Word became flesh' (John 1:1, 14).

B In the second sermon you can move to the First Christmas, to the First Advent, to Christmas Past, and your text might well be Galatians 4:4, and your theme would be that world long ago to which Christ came, and the unpropitious circumstances of his coming.

C The third sermon would be on Christmas Present, Advent Now – now is the appointed time, now is the day of salvation; be like those who watch – *that* is the note, and the aim is to help your people to recover the expectation of Christmas. There are many suitable passages, parables, and texts as a basis for such a sermon. 'When the Son of man cometh, shall he find faith on the earth?' (Luke 18:8 KJV). Or one of the parables in Matthew 25.

D The Last Advent is the theme of the fourth sermon: what is loosely called the second coming. You want to get this into proper New Testament perspective for your people, not making either too little of it or too much, and recommending a proper agnosticism. You can quote Mark 13:32, showing that our Lord indicates that nobody knows the day or the hour, not even He knows. God knows.

• What is important is that the end, like the beginning, is under the control of the God we have seen definitively in Jesus Christ. Compare the great ending of Romans 8. Which text? – Romans 8:22.

IV For a fourth series let me simply give you telegraphically suggested ideas:

A Christ comes to the world.
B Christ comes to the nation.
C Christ comes to the Church.
D Christ comes to the individual.

Finally, I have already said about all I want to say about Christmas Eve, Christmas Day, and the service on the Sunday after Christmas, but in closing I would make two requests, one positive, the other negative.

The first is that you concentrate on the Christmas story as we have it in Luke's Gospel. This is a wondrous story, and in my experience, celebrating Christmas with my congregation for more than forty Christmases in different lands and in varying circumstances, it is a story which never grows stale and which is ever new. That is the positive request I would make.

The second and negative request is that you don't romanticise the nativity story. The shepherds were not romantic figures. They were ritually unclean persons. They not only worked unsocial hours, but they were regarded as rather unsociable characters. And a stable is a place that smells of dung. It's not romantic; it's squalid for a child to be born in a stable. And a baby is a creature that is smelly and needs its nappies changed. That is part of the real humanity of the Christ, and don't obscure that by Christmas-card romanticism, or by what Hans Kung calls the 'romantic ecclesiological love of the past'.

The wonder is that the love that is God came down in the person of a baby, and this was revealed to ordinary men and women, at their work, where they were and as they were. And if, as some commentators suggest, the birth stories are legendary, the fact is that much of history is legend, and those birth stories are nevertheless the vehicle of blessed truth.

2

EPIPHANY

THE season of the Christian Year which follows Advent and Christmas is called *Epiphany. Epiphany* is derived from a Greek word which means the manifestation, the coming of the light. In the words prefacing the suggested lessons for the Sundays in Epiphany in *The Worshipbook*, it is 'a season marking the revelation of God's gift of himself to all'.

I have found that this is a season which does not lend itself so readily to the preaching of a series of sermons, and that for various reasons.

For one thing, congregations, in my experience, appreciate two or three series of sermons in the year, but become restive if there are too many series of sermons. They like a break from the calculable and the expected. They prefer occasionally to be surprised, not to know what is coming next, and if you have just finished an Advent series preparing them for Christmas, and if you are going to have a series in Lent preparing them for Holy Week and Easter, then Epiphany, I suggest, is a time when you can dispense with an obvious and stated series. For another thing, Epiphany varies greatly in length according to how early or how late Easter falls. It begins on January 6 and continues until Ash Wednesday, which means that it may cover anything from four to nine Sundays.

But most important, Epiphany is a season that lends itself more to thematic than to seriatim treatment. The Epiphany theme is as great and diverse as the world and all the nations. 'The Gospel refers to an event which is "determinative not only for the [individual] human soul, but for nature and history in their totalities"' (Lesslie Newbigin, *The Finality of Christ* [Richmond: John Knox Press, 1969], p 55). Jesus Christ came not only to his own who received him not, but to a world which rejected him. He came for the world. The definitive synopsis of the gospel in John 3:16 significantly holds together the cosmic and the personal concern of God in Christ. That is the grand theme of Epiphany. And that theme is too big and too diverse to be easily comprised in some tidy scheme.

But I would not be dogmatic about this. If, for good reason, or none, you have not had an Advent series, it may be worthwhile on occasion to develop an Epiphany series; but never having done so myself, I would hesitate to suggest such a series.

What I would elaborate on is the diversity of the Epiphany theme of God and the world.

I   *It takes in the Creation*

Significantly, one of the Old Testament lessons suggested in this period is from the first chapter of Genesis. This provides the opportunity and the challenge of discussing with your people how they should regard the creation stories in Genesis. Are they true? Or are they full of truth? And is there not a real difference between those two questions? There is, I believe, a real difference, the blurring of which has caused a lot of needless distress. The Eastern mind clearly accepts the difference between those two questions much more readily than the Western mind which has had recourse to words like myth which have tended to mystify our people and caused us to be accused of doubletalk. You have the opportunity of clarifying your own mind on this question, and, having done that, of instructing the congregation on how to distil and extract the great relevant truths in the creation stories.

My own mind was much influenced by the experience of living for eight years in Africa and being exposed to the African way of communicating truth. That way uses story and imagery rather than concepts. It is neither a superior way nor an inferior way. It is simply a different way from our normal Western way. We have a nasty habit of imagining that if something is different from something else it must be inferior or superior. Value judgements of difference are often quite inappropriate.

The Bible is predominantly an Eastern book, and therefore a common method of communicating truth in the Bible is by story and imagery. We have no difficulty about this when we come to Jesus' parables – or at least not very much – but I would point out that Jesus does not say as preface to the parables: 'I'm going to tell you a story.' He says: 'A certain man had two sons.' He says: 'A certain man went down from Jerusalem to Jericho, and fell among thieves.' Normally we have no difficulty in the parables in seeing the distinction between truth and the story, between what is being communicated and the method of communication. I do recall, however, that on the Jerusalem-to-Jericho road, when the busload of pilgrims I was with stopped at an inn called 'The Good Samaritan', one lady asked me in awed tones: 'Was this the inn that the Good Samaritan took the man to?'

I said, 'Well, we generally think of it as a parable.'

She said, 'Of course, how stupid of me.'

'Not at all, this is one occasion, and it is not the only one, when Jesus did not begin, "Here is the writer of the gospel. Here is a parable".'

And in the course of dealing with the creation stories, you have an opportunity of disabusing the minds of your people about some of the commonly held notions about evolution. For example, the notion that evolutionary theory remains where Darwin left it in *The Origin of Species,* or indeed the notion that there is one agreed theory of evolution at all. Some years before he died I asked Dr Louis Leakey, the distinguished anthropologist who lived and worked in Africa, what Vailleton, the French biologist, might have meant when he said that 'the word creation which had been removed from the biological dictionary would have to be brought back'. And, I asked him, did he agree with the statement. In his answer he explained that Darwin had postulated a development or evolution of species which was automatic, one thing followed naturally from another. And Darwin produced brilliant evidence. But Darwin acknowledged not just one missing link – the one between us and the higher apes – but many missing links which he was confident his successors would in time discover and so confirm and complete the picture of a natural, automatic evolution. 'But,' said Dr Leakey, 'this has not happened, and we think there have been enough people engaged on this task and enough time to look for those missing links if they were there to be found, and we have looked but we haven't found them'. He went on to say two things: one, that there was clearly evolution, a species appeared and evolved but then a new species appeared. There was apparently a gap between species – and what, he said, he could only describe as a creative burst occurred between species. This was, he believed, what Vailleton meant by saying that the word creation had to be restored to their vocabulary. Second, Dr Leakey, who was by the way a reverent agnostic, said that he was always astonished at the degree of accuracy, according to their present knowledge, in the sequence of creation pictured in the creation accounts in the book of Genesis. Dr Leakey died a few years ago. I regarded it as an honour to be invited to review the book on his life.

You would, of course, be mainly concerned to emphasise the comforting theological truth that from beginning to end the world is God's world. 'The earth is the LORD'S and the fullness thereof' (Psalm 24:1). But it is not unimportant to debunk the notion that somehow or other Darwin or science or someone has successfully bowed God out of the cosmic process. This is a common notion, and it does worry people. They are very uncomfortable about that idea. As much as anything this is also what lies behind one of the most common questions on lips today: 'What is the world coming to?'

The discoveries that have taken place in our lifetime, the continuing examination of the universe, in minuscule or majuscule, the explorations into space, are on balance working for us, or can be shown to be on the side of faith, though I should not need to caution you that a faith based on science is built on shifting sands. By its very nature the discoveries and theories of science change. All I am suggesting is that the discoveries of science are not always – as they are too often assumed to be – inimical to faith. And you should demonstrate that when you are dealing with this world and this universe, this creation of the almighty Creator. On the other hand the church, almost throughout its history, has not always been prepared to listen and to accept new truth from the past to the present day.

Space exploration, for example, can have an ambivalent effect on our minds. On the one hand a universe in which, as one astrophysicist has put it, 'there are as many stars in the universe as there are grains of sand on all the seashores of the world', is awesome and daunting. The thought that the light of the stars we look at twinkling away may have taken centuries to reach us, and that those stars may have been extinguished hundreds of years ago, gives some idea, a *mind-boggling* idea, of the vastness of space. The fact that we can now not only find our way in those vast spaces, but can make a rendezvous timed to the second with other space explorers at a point in that vastness, says something not just about our own competence and cleverness, but about the orderliness, calculability and reliability of the universe. It says something – not too much and not enough – about the reality behind it all that we call God. It is only those of faith, like the psalmist poet, who can say:

He heals the broken hearted,
and binds up their wounds.
He determines the number of the stars,
he gives to all of them their names. (Psalm 147:3-4)

It is only faith, the faith that is revealed in Christ, that can see and believe that that is the true marvel, that the God behind the universe is one who both counts the stars and is concerned with us in our brokenness, to help and to heal. This is, of course, the great, significant message of the prologue to St John's Gospel.

II *This comprehensiveness of God's concern for his whole creation and for the individual obviously includes within it the world of nations, both international and national.*

From cover to cover, both in the Old Testament and in the New, God is seen as being concerned with history. Isaiah is the great prophet of history, but in the earlier historical books God's concern is clearly for Israel, for the making of a nation, and the saving of a nation, though not exclusively so. He is the God of Israel, but he is the God of Israel because he is the God of all the earth, and at least part of his concern for Israel is because: 'You only have I known of – and made myself known to – all the families [*ie* nations] of the earth; therefore' – you are specially favoured, and my favourite is reserved for super-generous treatment? Not so – 'therefore I will punish you' (Amos 3:2).

This means that Epiphany is a period when you may very properly deal with the contemporary international world in the light of the insights of the Bible, and in particular in the light of the coming of Christ as the Light of the World. The important message which people need reassurance about is that God is concerned with the world of nations. The corollary of that is that so must we be concerned. As Christians this is part of our duty to God and to neighbour. The Christian cannot be an isolationist. Like others, we may not know enough about international situations to make assured judgments, but we have a duty to become as well informed as we can and to apply to the world scene judgments which are informed and which are guided by the values and the spirit which we have seen brought down to earth and incarnated in Jesus Christ.

It must never be forgotten – nor must you allow your people to forget – that it was into an international world, and as a member of a particular race and nation, that Christ came. It was to a real world – in contrast to the tinsel world so often presented at Christmas – that the Son of God came. It was to a world of poverty and of housing shortage; it was to a world whose institutions were corrupt and in decay, a corruption and a decay that he protested against, that he denounced, that he came to save from going utterly to the bad; it was to a world of tyrannies and taxes, of politics and finance; it was a world in which there was injustice and cruelty, a world that knew not the things that belonged to its peace.

The Evangelists are aware of all that. The significance of the genealogy at the beginning of Matthew's Gospel – despite the artificiality and dubiousness that is a feature of almost all genealogies which go back, as this one claims, no less than 42 generations – is that it is saying that God has a plan. He is Alpha and Omega, the beginning and the end, and that the coming of Jesus is central to history and at the same time that all those people, most of them just names and some completely unknown, have had a part in God's plan and purpose. So have you.

It is into a real world, a historical world, a world of empire and nations, of power blocs and politics, that Christ comes.

This is the significance of the beginning of the second chapters of Matthew and Luke. It was when Caesar Augustus was the emperor and Rome was the great world power, when Quirinius was governor of Syria, when Herod was king of Judea and when there was an imperial census, that Jesus was born. It was into the context of history. Not for nothing do the most ancient of the Church's creeds include the words 'suffered under Pontius Pilate' among the essentials of the faith. It happened in history. It continues now.

Epiphany properly celebrated is saying not just that, but that Jesus Christ still sheds his light over this world, and that as he is eternally involved in its affairs so must his Church and so must individual Christians be involved in challenging the darknesses, our warring nationalisms, our racism, our toleration of continuing injustices, our low political standards or complete lack of them, our power blocs, our historical and historic decisions.

This is a difficult and a perilous task. In his unpublished autobiography, a friend, Robert Macpherson, has this to say:

In the area of seeking to influence public affairs, the defects of the Church's witness have been ... striking. To say this is not to deprecate the Church's being concerned with public issues. As a continuing society within a wider community it is bound to become involved. But it is a part of its witness that is fraught with deadly peril for its well-being .... It has in the past, for example ... often lent its authority to activities which were an open denial of the gospel which sustains it. We may note the Crusades, the Civil Wars, the pogroms, the Inquisitions and other abuses of authority which it has pursued from time to time over the centuries. In more modern times it can rightly be reproached for its tacit or overt concordats with oppressive regimes of both right and left, its tolerance of race and class prejudice – and its too-ready support of 'righteous wars'.

But we must also note that over the centuries it has not been allowed to lose its identity as a vehicle of divine grace. Overall it can be said that it was instrumental in redeeming and transforming the ancient world. Later, when that world was overrun by barbarians, it was again largely instrumental in preserving the Christian heritage and the tradition of civilisation and law to which the ancient world had attained. And it has sought to maintain a witness against oppression and cruelty into modern times. It is also true, I think, that where society has tried, however imperfectly, to support those values to which the Church aspires, it has remained to that degree stable. And where it has rejected them ... the floodgates of evil then seem to open and threaten to engulf that society in what Jung once called 'a torrent of libido, lust, cruelty and greed'. Such a cycle of events has taken place in Britain over the past fifty years.

There is little I would find to disagree with in that. It is not without significance that it was on a political-cum-religious charge that our Lord was condemned and crucified. Significantly, the charge in three international languages was nailed to his cross: 'The King of the Jews.' It is of paramount importance that your people should be educated by you to recognise that our God is God of all the earth, that he is concerned with this world in its ongoing and its goings on, here and now, so concerned that he sent his Son to save it from perishing, and that that concern is not finished when it is done.

It is important that this should be pointed out to your people as theological fact based on biblical truth and quite independently of any particular issue of the moment, for if you fail to get that across to them, then, when you do come to apply this general and all-embracing truth to some particular international, national, or community issue on which, in God's name, you feel called to speak, you will find that many will avoid applying their Christian judgment to the matter because it never occurred to them that their faith had anything to do with the real world beyond the narrow confines of their individual and family life.

At the same time I would point out that it is not the business of the pulpit to give a running commentary Sunday by Sunday on the week's news, but it is your business to help your people to realise that it is their business to apply the criterion, who is Christ, to the totality of human affairs; and, as I have said, there are occasions when you will have to give your people specific guidance on matters of moment. Or you will fail them. But remember, if you are forever going off like a popgun people are not likely to pay much attention when some really important issue comes up with which you have to deal and in which they will look to you to give a lead. And even if you have nothing to say about some national or international issue you can commend the issue to God in prayers. If you do, don't tell God what he has to do!

III *Epiphany is also a time when we have an opportunity of emphasising the responsibility of the Church for mission and for calling for commitment to this duty without the distraction of calling for cash.*

There has been a loss of confidence in mission in the last two or three decades. There are reasons for that. In part it has been due to a proper distaste for a patronising and paternalistic attitude which lay behind some expressions of our missionary enterprise in the earlier part of this century. In part, in Britain to a considerable extent, and in America to a lesser extent, it is due to a feeling that since we no longer have an imperial responsibility for other peoples we have no missionary responsibility. To some extent the missionary followed the flag, though historically in several places the missionary was there before the flag, and in the providence of God the Church is there after the flag has been lowered and another flag hoisted. In part, the decline and diffidence about the Church's mission to the world is due to a doubt about whether we are wanted. But perhaps the major cause of the decline in zeal for mission is a lack of confidence in the supreme value of the Christian faith. Popularly this is expressed in questions like: 'These people have their own faith, haven't they? Why should we try to impose our faith?' Theologically this is an expression of doubt in the Lordship of Christ and in the faith that he is God's only Son, God's last word which – yes, together with those of other faiths and of none – we have still fully to understand and to explore and to implement.

But the claim of the faith is that he is the Light of the World. That is not to say that there is no light in other faiths of other people, but if we believe that in him the true light now shines we have a duty in word and in deed to proclaim that to the whole world.

Increasingly, the Church and the churches are realising that the mission of the Church is one. The old division between home and foreign mission is seen as artificial. In part this is because as never before in history we are aware that we are citizens of the world and that the world is a global village. In part, however slowly, we are beginning to recognise and to accept that we are members one of another. We live, and our lives are enriched by the international commerce of the world. There is – and this is encouraging for those who accept the great commission to go into all the world and proclaim the good news – among the world religions an openness to the Christian faith today which is one of the newer features of the religious world scene. True, there are the dangers of agnosticism and the temptation to make too easy accommodations and compromises with other faiths, which in the end are far from helpful to the establishment of the kingdom of God and less than honest to the holders of other faiths. This, however, provides an opportunity for mission which ought not to be missed.

Of course, the immediate responsibility for mission rests with the Young Churches (where these are established), but we ought still to be fellow workers with them, and they ought to be increasingly fellow workers with us in the mission which is our immediate responsibility where we are. Some years ago, when I visited Ghana and Nigeria in West Africa, among the requests made to me by the Church was a proposal that they should send three or four of their best ministers and we should send three or four of our best ministers to work in each other's country for an extended period of at least a year, in order that we might both learn from each other and help each other towards a fuller understanding of our mission. We are living in a world in which the nations are rubbing shoulders together as never before. We believe that in the Christian faith we have the matrix and recipe for a common life of one humanity in the one God and Father of us all. In a thousand ways, here, there and everywhere, we must both preach and practice this faith. This is the Church's business and therefore your business. Wasn't it Brunner who said that the Church lives by mission as a fire lives by burning? As Jesus himself said: 'As the Father has sent me [into the world], even so I send you' (John 20:21).

IV *But what has all this – our doctrine of the universe and our world, our concern with the problems of society and the business of learning to live together, we who belong to different races and colours and who speak different languages and yet are one humanity, and our obligation to proclaim to the whole world the nature of the one God revealed in Christ – got to do with the simple starting point of Epiphany which is the story of the coming of the Wise Men? The answer is: just about everything.*

This, wherever you may end, is where you must begin with the Epiphany message. The story of the coming of the Wise Men, containing legendary elements, as all history does, is one of the most meaningful stories in the New Testament, and if it is read with Christian imagination almost every detail of it is significant. Even what we don't know is significant.

They came vaguely from the East. We don't know from how far away east of Jordan they came. Old legend has further added that they were from three continents and of three racial groups – Aryan, African, and Asiatic. They have even been given names going back to the twelfth century – Caspar, Melchior, and Balthazar. And it has been suggested that they represented three age groups – Caspar an old man, Melchior a middle-aged man, and Balthazar a young man. Persistent legend often reflects deep insight, and this legendary material indicates the conviction that came home to human imagination that the coming of Jesus was for the whole world, for all races, and for all ages. Sometimes, as you know, legend contains more truth than what is contained in and selected from the mass of facts which is called history.

Does the fact that we do not know where the Wise Men came from – we don't even know how many there were, the number three is no doubt a deduction from the three varieties of gifts they brought and gave to the child at Bethlehem – does the fact that we know so little about them not remind us that we still are very ignorant about our neighbours, near or far? No man is an island, but every man is in some sense a foreigner to every other. We are all to some degree unknown to and separate from one another. The story of the Wise Men suggests what I believe is profoundly true, that we meet when we engage together in the active quest for the fullest revelation of God with the intention together of worship and commitment to that reality whose chiefest quality is caring for all. The more we know of the divine the more we believe.

That does not mean that we are all led unerringly. Even the Wise Men looked at first in a seemingly likely quarter for the newborn king. Where else but in a king's palace? Where else but in our political institutions should we look for our salvation, to our parliaments, and our pacts, and our international organisations? But they, wise as they were, were wrong. Salvation was not to be found where they thought it might be.

And notice this, further, that those in the place of power, the advisers to authority, knew where they should look for salvation. They had heard it long ago. It was written into their records, and they could say that it was in Bethlehem of Judea that the Christ, the Lord, the Governor, was to be born. But they didn't look there. They didn't go there. It had become a dead tradition and not a living hope.

'The powers that be are ordained of God' (Romans 13:1, KJV) – we have the authority of Scripture for saying so, but constantly we have to recall wise men who are saying, 'Let us go to Washington or London or the United Nations or some other place to find the answer to our hunger for peace and a solution to our problems'. And we have all, first, to follow the pinpoint of light we have before us and to say, with simple shepherds, 'Let us now go even unto Bethlehem' (Luke 2:15, KJV). One of the most heartening things about the contemporary scene which is implicit in the story of the coming of the Wise Men is that, in the deepest sense, those of different nations and of different religions are, even out of a desperate distrust of their own wisdom and competence, beginning to do just that, and in a very real sense are becoming convinced that Jesus Christ is the revelation of the reality behind the world, and that to ignore that means that our world lies broken and on the very edge of ultimate disaster and disintegration.

I do not say that there would be universal agreement about putting what they feel into those words, but I am convinced that that is the growing feeling; and that places a great responsibility on the Church and on you to point everyone the way to find the Christ and to interpret what that means for the world. And always with respect for those of other faiths in mind.

That is not to say that there will not always be those who, at any cost, will apply themselves to the attempted destruction of all the potential that God through Christ is always seeking to bring to birth in the world. There will always be those who see, and rightly see, the Christ as a threat to themselves and to things as they are and who will cruelly slaughter the innocents if only they can prevent him. There is always the shadow of the cross falling on the crib. The cost of the attempt to silence the Christ is always borne by innocent humanity.

But here again the lesson of the story is that the Christ escapes the evil designs of those who would harm him, though there is still to come the deeper lesson of the cross. The ultimate triumph of God in Christ is through the cross to resurrection. The Christ escapes to die upon a cross in order that he might rise to live forever.

Much has been made, and many are the interpretations given, about the gifts of gold, frankincense, and myrrh which the Wise Men are reported to have brought. There may be a convenient three-decker sermon there, though I would have thought that it might more fittingly serve as the raw material for a children's address, or at the most a paragraph in a sermon rather than the whole subject. The main point, and one that is relevant to our time, is surely that here in symbol we have the dedication by Wise Men of their individual gifts to the Christ child and all that he in the intention of God means to the world. We have more often as a Church offended – and not least offended those with great gifts, both intellectual and material – by not expecting enough of them rather than by expecting or demanding too much. The Church has been impoverished materially and even more intellectually by our hesitation concerning and our suspicion of the wealthy and the wise. Our relationship with and attitude to the scientist – and the Wise Men may properly be regarded as primitive scientists – have been at best uneasy and at worst unsympathetic. The Church has nothing to fear from the honest inquiries, questing, and questioning of the scientist. This is another area that might very well be explored during Epiphany. The differences and the relationship between the scientific methods of discovery and the ways of finding where ultimate truth is to be found are too seldom tackled and teased out. Our continuing failure to do so may give the impression that scientific methods are the only valid ways of arriving at truth, and in a technological age in which the educational system leans heavily on scientific methods, the results in the long run are an impoverishment of all in the things of the spirit. We will produce a race of intellectual, or rather scientific, giants, but moral and spiritual dwarfs. And, at least in part, the fault is the fault of the Church – its suspicion, its fear, its lack of welcome and encouragement, its failure to call wise men to follow the glimmer of light wherever it may lead them and to bring their various gifts and to make their homage to God in Christ to the service of humanity. The kingdom of God has suffered from this failure.

One last point before we leave Epiphany and the Wise Men. Part of the story which is commonly neglected, but which is meaningful, is what happened after they had presented their gifts and done homage to the infant king. Too often the tableaux and the sermon leave the Wise Men, contrary to the New Testament, with the shepherds and in the stable, which may be permissible as dramatic license; but in fact, as the New Testament account tells us, it was some time after the birth of Jesus that the Wise Men came. The New Testament indicates that they had been some time on the journey and that it was in a house that they found the child and his mother. But it goes on to tell us that they didn't stay there, and I would urge you to have at least one sermon devoted not to the coming of the Wise Men, but to the *return* of the Wise Men. I would even dare to suggest some of the points you might make.

You might begin by frankly confessing that too often we leave the Wise Men at the end of their journey, as if that was an end in itself. It wasn't, and it never is. And it ought not to be.

You might go on to point out that they returned to their own country, and we all have to return from our worship to our own place.

But they went lighter. They had offered their gifts and themselves. I wonder if we realise what a burden those who acquire or are endowed with material wealth, secular power, or intellectual gifts have to carry. You have a word of wisdom for them here in the example of the returning Wise Men who had dedicated their gifts and went back with a lighter load in consequence.

There is also the dream. Don't be sidetracked by the temptation to inform the congregation about the work that has been done this century on the significance of dreams, interesting and important and to some extent relevant to this story as that may be. The significance for them and for us is that companying with the Christ gave them and should give us a sensitivity to what is evil, that will help us to bypass it. On the way there they knew no better than to go to Herod's palace. On the way back they did not go back to Herod but returned to their own country another way.

And that leads me to another point. They kept in touch with the Christian community that grew up and was centred on the Christ who was and always is both the end and the beginning of our quest. I deduce this from the fact that the Evangelist records their return, the account of the dream, and the bypassing of Herod. The report of their coming could have been from a Mary source, from her account. But the subsequent story, their going, their dream, the avoidance of Herod, their safe return, could only have come from the Wise Men and from some continuing communication with the community that the coming of Jesus began. And there is a lesson, if we are wise, for all of us, in that.

Laurence Housman's hymn 'Father Eternal, Ruler of Creation' (362 in *The Worshipbook*) should be the prayer of the Church at Epiphany:

Father eternal, Ruler of creation,
Spirit of life, which moved ere form was made;
Through the thick darkness covering every nation,
Light to man's blindness, O be now our aid:
Your kingdom come, O Lord, your will be done.

Races and peoples, lo! we stand divided,
And sharing not our griefs, no joy can share;
By wars and tumults Love is mocked, derided,
His conquering cross no kingdom wills to bear:
Your kingdom come, O Lord, your will be done.

Envious of heart, blind-eyed, with tongues confounded,
Nation by nation still goes unforgiven;
In wrath and fear, by jealousies surrounded,
Building proud towers which shall not reach to heaven:
Your kingdom come, O Lord, your will be done.

How shall we love you, holy, hidden Being,
If we love not the world which you have made?
O give us brother-love for better seeing
Your Word made flesh, and in a manger laid:
Your kingdom come, O Lord, your will be done.

3

LENT

THE season of Lent which follows Epiphany is the forty week-days and six Sundays which begin on Ash Wednesday and end with Palm Sunday and the beginning of Holy Week. This chapter will deal with the main themes which have traditionally governed the Church's thinking and worship during this period – up to, but not including, Palm Sunday, which I will take up in the next chapter, which will be devoted to preaching in Holy Week.

The mood of Lent is suggested by the lessons in *The Worshipbook* for Ash Wednesday and, since I have never preached on Ash Wednesday, and I suspect that you are not likely to be called on to do so, I should explain that I am directing your attention to those lessons because I think it is important that we should get what I have called 'the mood of Lent' right.

I simply take one of the three sets of lessons proposed in *The Worshipbook* for Ash Wednesday to illustrate what that mood is. The lessons (p 169) are Joel 2:12-18; 2 Corinthians 5:20-6:2; and Matthew 6:1-6, 16-18. The keynote of the Joel passage is in the familiar text, 'rend your heart, and not your garments', which is a reference to the ancient custom of expressing anguish and sorrow by the almost hysterical tearing of clothes. The term Ash Wednesday is, of course, a reference to another ritual gesture denoting grief – the wearing of sackcloth and the throwing of ashes on the head and smearing the face with them. You find several examples of this practice in the Old Testament, in Isaiah and Jonah and Daniel, to mention only three of the books that refer to this act expressing, in an outward form, deep distress. The distress to which Ash Wednesday refers is sorrow over sin, and one of the points which individually and collectively the lessons from Joel, from Corinthians and from the Gospel emphasise is that this distress must be not so much an outward show but an inward sense. 'Rend your heart, and not your garments.' In Corinthians Paul is proclaiming the inward working of God's grace in Christ who, innocent of sin himself, for our sake is made one with sinners, so that in him we might be made one with the goodness of God. In the passage in Matthew, chapter 6, our Lord discourages the mere outward show, whether it be announcing your love of your neighbour with a flourish or proclaiming your pious familiarity with God by public prayer, or protesting your repentance and sorrow for the sins of the world and your own by your gaunt and gloomy expression and a dirty face (a reference to the use of ashes to smear the face). Wash your face, he says, shampoo your hair, and show both people and God a fair appearance – something which is more difficult for some than for others! – even while inwardly your heart is heavy with an awareness of personal unworthiness and you are burdened with a sense of the exceeding sinfulness of sin.

The word 'Lent' comes from an Old English word meaning Spring, and it may be significant that in Lent there is a parallelism between the natural and the spiritual season. Certainly the one is in tune with the other. Spring is the mixed season. It is the period of lengthening days, when the dark is giving way to the light. It is a time when the cold earth is beginning to be warmed and signs of new life are appearing. It is a time of weeping skies but with the sun breaking through, a time of showers and sunshine. It is a mixed season but a season that we know is going to lead to the joy of summer and the triumph of a world risen from the apparent death of Winter.

Spiritually, Lent is a similar season to Spring. Contrary to common ideas it is not a time of unrelieved gloom. Even if we accept the discipline of some outward expression of spiritual training by giving up some pleasure, the equivalent of fasting, and applying the proceeds of our self-denial to some good cause, there should be a healthy glow related to, and a consequence of, the discipline, and the more rigorous the discipline the greater the glow.

We have to make clear to people what the great words associated with Lent really mean, and we may have to begin by correcting some common misunderstandings. I mention, as examples, four of the words which should be much on our lips at this season, words which represent the main themes of Lent.

The first is *temptation.* I will be dealing with this in a homiletic way, outlining how this theme might be tackled when you come to deal with it in your preaching.

All I want to emphasise here is a point that is obvious when it is made, but which requires to be made even though it is a negative point: temptation is not sin and should not be confused with sin. Our Lord was tempted. The account of his temptations form the Gospel lessons for the first Sunday in Lent. Our Lord was tempted and his temptation was severe, but our Lord resisted the temptation. Our Lord was without sin.

The second is *sin.* I think it is because we cannot say – about ourselves or anyone – that we are without sin; that there has been a pessimistic tendency to assume that temptation and sin, if not exactly the same, lead to the same thing in the end – sinfulness. True, and yet not simply true. Temptation is not the same as sin. We are called to resist temptation even if the resistance draws blood. We are taught in the model prayer to pray that we may not be led into temptation, and you will find from time to time that you have to deal with people who are tormented by temptation and part of whose torment is that they have failed to distinguish between temptation and sin.

At the same time we have to recognise, and we have to tell people, that to dally with temptation, to flirt and linger with temptation, leads to a borderline between temptation and sin which at times is indistinguishable. I believe that this is the point of our Lord's words in the Sermon on the Mount about looking on a woman with a lustful eye being well on the way to adultery of the heart. You can fantasise temptation to such an extent that it becomes sin. And you have to be wise to yourself and you have to help your people to be wise to themselves while at the same time emphasising the difference between temptation and sin.

Similarly there is a difference between *repentance* and remorse. Repentance is the second great word on our lips, and more, in our hearts, during Lent. Is it not true that we commonly think of repentance in a negative way, as a dust-and-ashes affair? I am inclined to think that this is so because we do confuse it with remorse, with merely being sorry. Remorse is the most negative and potentially destructive of all sensations, and there's a lot of truth in the saying that it's no use being sorry.

Many people are eaten by remorse and feel genuinely sorry for what they have done and for what they are, but while that may lead to repentance it is a hopeless business if it doesn't.

The accent of the Bible, and especially of the New Testament, is on the positive aspect of repentance. The commonest Greek word for repentance, *metanoia,* means renewal, a change, a transformation of the heart and mind, leading to a new life. It is there that the accent must fall. It is this that is good news for us sinners, that repentance is a positive possibility, and that not simply by our own efforts but by the grace and long-suffering love of God revealed and assured to us in Jesus Christ.

It is your duty and your delight to make that clear in your preaching on this theme. Just as God constantly and repeatedly renews the face of the earth at Springtime, so he constantly and repeatedly comes with renewal to us. That is the divine aspect of repentance, and that is God's doing, and it is wonderful in our eyes. If in Springtime you preach on a romantic text like: 'For, lo, the winter is past, the rain is over and gone; the flowers appear on the earth; the time of the singing of birds is come' (Song of Solomon 2:11-12, KJV), don't get too carried away – you may find on the Sunday morning that it's lashing with rain and the whole world is sad and sodden! – but above all drive home the hopeful truth of repentance as an integral part of the gospel. That is the spring of hope.

The third word that, along with temptation and repentance, makes up the trio of key words of the Lenten season is *sin.*

Over sixty years ago, when I was studying psychology in my first degree, we had a weekly practical class in experimental psychology. One of the common experiments was the monitoring of reaction times to the stimulus of given words. We worked in pairs and took turns feeding each other with a list of words. On a given word, the person being fed the word had to reply with the first word that came to mind, and the person given the word recorded by means of a stopwatch the reaction time. If the reaction time was much slower than average, the theory was that the delay was caused by the time taken even subconsciously to get rid of the first word that was coming up and substituting another word. In a class of about fifty, when we tabulated the results, we found that there was a slow reaction time in almost every case in response to the word 'sin'. Consciously or subconsciously, we all have a sense of sin, and our guilt weighs us down and slows us up.

As ministers you will have to deal with the sin-burdened and their particular sins. You will also have to deal with the sins of society, with our class sins and our race sins and our national sins, for there are corporate sins, though the Church and ministers have often been more conscious of corporal than corporate sins. You must not treat the fact of sin too lightly or minimise the cost of sin. After all, we are moving in this Lenten season towards the cross, which is the condemnation of sin and the expression of the cost of sin.

But here again you have some corrective work to do. You not only have to say something about the origin of sin. How came sin in a world which at its beginning God looked on and saw it good? Here you must wrestle with the problem of humanity, made in the image of God, yet rightly guilt-laden and marred by sin. There are occasions of disaster that your people will recognise as the consequence of sin but will still ask: 'If God is almighty could he not have prevented sin and its consequence, and in particular that consequence?' And you will have to point out that God is more almighty as a Creator of human beings who are free than he would be if all he could make were puppets. And if we are really free we are free to sin, and we have. 'All have sinned and come short of the glory of God.'

The delayed reaction time is a sign that deep down we know that. But notice that here again there is a hopeful side to this truth. To know that we are fallen means that there is a higher destiny for which we are predestined. From time to time in our courts, psychologists will give evidence that an accused has no sense of guilt or shame, no awareness of wrong done, no responsibility, and this is regarded as a great horror, as something almost inhuman and, in extreme cases, the certification may be that the person concerned is insane. It is commonly accepted that it is not unhealthy, but on the contrary a healthy sign, to have a sense of sin. Thank God for it, for if you have it you are normal.

You will, of course, point people to one of the great doctrines of the Church which finds its way into the oldest of the creeds: 'I believe in the forgiveness of sins.'

The fourth great Lenten theme is *forgiveness*. One of the great attributes of the grace of God is his mercy. The story is told of Alexander Whyte, the great preacher and churchman who flourished at the beginning of this century, minister of Free St George's, Edinburgh, and Principal of the Free Church College – a stern, bushy-eyebrowed, formidable character. He had visited an old man who, unknown to Whyte, was burdened and depressed by his sense of sin. As he was leaving, the old man turned to him and asked: 'Have you a word for a sinful old man?' Dr Whyte looked at him through his bushy eyebrows and said, quoting from the prophet Micah: 'He delighteth in mercy' (7:18, KJV). The man wrote him a letter that night to say how that word had cheered him and lifted him out of his distress. It is a word which you have a duty and which it is your privilege to proclaim. It is a word sealed with the cross of Christ.

I want to look now in greater detail at some of the Lenten passages from the Gospels which are suggested in the lectionary. Some of them are passages that present problems which you will have to face with your congregation. We will touch on some of those problems.

The lesson for the first Sunday in Lent is about the temptation of Jesus which is elaborated in Matthew 4 and Luke 4. It is possible that the forty days of Lent are reminiscent of the forty days of fasting and temptation of our Lord described in the Gospels. I am going to look with you at the account in Matthew, which differs from Luke mainly in the order of the three temptations. In Matthew the order is first the temptation to make bread of stones, second the temptation in the highest and holiest place, the pinnacle of the Temple, and third the temptation to rule the world on condition that the devil is worshipped. In Luke the sequence of two and three are reversed: the temptation to rule the world and worship the devil comes before the temptation on the high place of the Temple. Psychologically I think Matthew's order is preferable, and it is Matthew's account that we will follow.

The temptation of Jesus is very significant. I wonder if you have appreciated that this passage almost more than any other passage in the Gospels is certainly autobiographical. Jesus was alone when he had that experience. Only he could have told his disciples about it. Jesus is not given to chattering about himself. He is not unduly introspective, nor does he do much in the way of disclosing his inner and private spiritual experiences. He is usually reticent, and this is the only occasion on which he extensively gives an account of a private and personal spiritual experience. I think we can conclude from that two things. One, that this had a profound meaning for Jesus; and two, that it was meant to have a deep significance for the disciples and for us.

But before we come to the meaning, let me just say a word about the form of Jesus' communication. It is always difficult to express a deep spiritual experience. And this was such an experience. This was a storm in the soul. A ministry for God to save the world was beginning. How was the campaign to be waged? There is more than one method of attack. What are the dangers, the advantages, and the disadvantages that have to be faced and balanced as we fight the good fight? Something of that, I suggest, was engaging our Lord's heart and mind and soul as he prepared, in the wilderness, and in private with God, for his public ministry which was about to begin. Later he wanted to tell his disciples, whom he was sending out on the same mission, about the basic temptations that he had met and that they and we would meet, and this is the form he chose for his self-disclosure to them. It is a mythical form. It is an Eastern form. It is full of symbol and imagery of great meaning. It is quite unnecessary to burden people with the notion that to believe in the temptation you have to believe in an actual appearance of the devil, with or without horns and a tail, having dialogue with Jesus. The temptations are real. They came to Jesus. They come to all of us at different times. They have to be constantly resisted.

Look at them. The first one is the temptation of the material: make bread out of these stones. To Jesus, hungry and fasting, the temptation comes. To Jesus, compassionate for the poor and the needy, the temptation comes. He needs bread; all of us need bread. Multiply the material and the need is satisfied. Perhaps you doubt if he could have done it, and perhaps even more you doubt the relevance of this temptation to his disciples and to us. Can we make bread of stones? My first parish was 90 per cent coalminers and their families. What else are miners mining coal from the depth of the earth to win their daily bread doing, but making bread of stones? My second parish was a shipbuilding parish on the Clyde, and what else are those who build the great steel ships fashioned from iron ore doing, but making bread of stones? My third parish had an area of farmland, and there I saw

70

basic slag and limestone being spread on fields which were to yield the grain literally to make bread. The truth is that it is always by sometimes complicated manipulation of earth's hard material that we win our bread. It is from this capability of ours and from our need and the felt need of the world that the temptation comes to believe that bread is all that matters. We still need to be told, and we still need to tell our materialistic world, the word of God that man does not live by bread alone.

Having resisted that temptation, Jesus confronts the second temptation: the temptation of the spiritual. And it is significant that this temptation is pictured as taking place in the highest and holiest place – on a pinnacle of the Temple. For it is when we have rejected the temptation of the material and are being at our most spiritual and evidencing our utter dependence, as we think, that this temptation comes to us: cast yourself down. Throw yourself utterly in faith, yes a reckless and dangerous faith, on God, and he will look after you. Repeat to yourself and proclaim to others, including the starving, 'Man does not live by bread alone', as if it meant 'Man does not live by bread at all'. This is a temptation which comes to us all at times. The comfortable, the foolish, and the fanatical are peculiarly susceptible to this temptation, and all of us can be seduced by comfort, and none of us are wise all the time, and we can all be affected, some more some less, by fanaticism. Fanaticism is also at times not so much the temptation of the faithful as an expression of despair. The answer of God's word is: you must not test God like that.

We have two opposing temptations pulling us in opposite directions and setting up tremendous tensions which Jesus felt and which we feel. How do we resolve this conflict between the material and the spiritual? It is an attempt to find a resolution of this conflict that leads properly to the third temptation, which is the temptation at any cost to resolve the conflict, to end the warfare and to win the world: it is the temptation of unquestioning obedience, in contemporary terms it is the temptation of totalitarianism, which is the very devil.

The devil is the master of disguise and takes many forms. The message is always the same: leave it to me, fall down and worship me, and I will give you the world. In our time the state is in danger of becoming the devil. In other times the Church has become the devil. In some places the master race, of one colour or another, is the very devil. And always and everywhere you can look in your mirror and see the devil. 'I' ... 'I will decide' ... 'I alone will rule. Okay!'

So we have thought in weariness at the tensions and temptations which confront us, and always the word is: no. 'You shall worship the Lord your God and him only shall you serve.' That was the answer Jesus gave. It is never an easy answer. It meant the cross, but it is the only answer that leads to eternal life in this world and in the world to come.

May I suggest before leaving this great passage that you might do well to consider a series of four sermons on *temptation,* the first on temptation in general and then one each on the three temptations. There is enough material for three sermons in the passage.

On the other hand, or some other year, you might consider a series on the other great Lenten theme, *repentance.* Again an introductory sermon might be appropriate on the nature, need, and possibility of repentance. Such a series was broadcast by the BBC one year in Lent. I remember it because I preached one of the sermons in the series. As I recall, the four themes were:

- Repentance of the Individual.
- Repentance of the State.
- Repentance of the Church.
- Repentance of God.

And as for *sin,* you should require very little guidance about preaching on the fact of sin, though I would counsel you to avoid the scolding note or a self-righteous tone. Remember all have sinned and come short of the glory of God, but above all remember that it is seldom news to people that they are sinners. What is news, and what they need to be convinced of, is the forgiveness of God.

I recall that one year, by taking in the last two Sundays in Epiphany, I did preach a series of sermons on the Seven Deadly Sins. It's a mistaken idea that you must stick rigidly to the divisions of the Christian Year or, for that matter, to the lectionary. On the other hand, don't despise the opportunity given by the Christian Year or by the lectionary of dealing naturally and dispassionately, and as it comes, with difficult subjects or particular issues that might emerge – for example, in sermons on repentance of the state, or of the Church.

Nor must you evade difficult passages – for example, the one on Christ's transfiguration, which is one of the lessons suggested for the second Sunday in Lent. What a picture that is of our Lord in conference with Moses, the representative of the law, and with Elijah, the representative of the prophets, and himself the reconciler of both! We have in the Church and in the churches those who incline to the law, who talk, sometimes too easily, of the Christian Attitude, of Christian Morality, of Christian Values, of Christian Civilisation, as if there was a ready-mix recipe for all occasions – which there is not. And at the same time we always have in the Church and in the churches those who are prophetically critical and even contemptuous of all that, who would live by the Spirit, who seek freedom from the restrictive and, as they see it, blinkered moralities of the law, whose cry is, 'Love God and do what you like' – Augustine of Hippo's catchphrase, in apparent support of a Christian permissiveness. The transfiguration is, I believe, about that issue and about Christ glorified in the reconciliation of both points of view. And don't miss our Lord's refusal to give permanence to the solution, and instead, pragmatically leading his disciples down to earth where a distracted father was waiting with a demented child. Another passage which presents some difficulty is one of the lessons suggested for the third Sunday in Lent, the account of the marriage in Cana of Galilee and the water turned into wine – 120 gallons for a village wedding where they had already drunk freely! Is the message here, as A M Hunter suggests, that Jesus is saying in effect, 'This is the meaning of my whole ministry – it is changing water into wine?' I wonder what you would make of that passage in a sermon. It is worth pointing out that we only have the polite comment by one person – 'this is the best wine' – and no record that one gallon, far less 120, were turned into wine!

I believe you would find another passage from St John which is also suggested as a lesson for the third Sunday in Lent somewhat easier. It is the lesson about the woman of Samaria and Jesus' conversation with her at the well. That is a fascinating passage which reveals how radical Jesus was. Here you find him crossing the barriers which we still encounter and have still not wholly solved.

- There is the barrier of race – Jesus was a Jew, the woman was a Samaritan.
- There is the barrier of sex – Jesus was a man, she was quite a woman.
- There is the barrier of religion – the Jews and the Samaritans had traditional religious differences which divided them – 'Jews have no dealings with Samaritans' (John 4:9).

I have already emphasised that one of the advantages of following a lectionary and the Christian Year is that it brings you naturally to deal with difficult issues and to educate your congregation in what is Christ's way before the matter has become a burning issue or a bandwagon. I make no apology for repeating the advice and for illustrating what I mean from this passage. Here you can say something obviously Christian, on the basis of this dialogue, about race, women's liberation, and religious differences.

There are, of course, half a dozen sermons in this passage. It is one of many passages in the Bible to which you can return again and again. When you do, I think you will always find something new in it to share with your congregation.

You will find that passages of dialogue or interviews in Scripture, the confrontation of personalities, is a very useful source of sermon material. People are interested in people, and the people of the Bible are real people. Some examples from the Old Testament: the confrontation between Joseph and his brothers in Egypt when Joseph tells them who he is: 'it was not you who sent me here but God' (Genesis 45:8). A kindly intentioned predestination? Then there is the confrontation between David and Nathan after the Bathsheba affair. Nathan's parable of the ewe lamb and his 'Thou art the man' (II Samuel 12:7, KJV). There is the Daniel passage on the burning fiery furnace and the brave witness of the condemned men (Daniel 3:13-18). And there are many others. In the New Testament, in addition to the one already mentioned, there is the Nicodemus dialogue (John 3:1-15). There are the various disputations with the lawyers and the scribes and the Pharisees. There is the confrontation with Thomas and with Peter after Easter. And, of course, there are several in the book of Acts which you can draw upon.

Don't overdo this line of preaching, but don't dismiss it as too simple. We learn from other people, how they act and react, and above all we learn how God acts on and with people and often through people.

Another passage giving an account of a dialogue and disputation which is suggested for the fourth Sunday in Lent, is the ninth chapter of John. This begins with the disciples' question to Jesus about the man who was blind from birth: 'Who sinned,' they asked, 'this man or his parents, that he was born blind?'

This is a passage which raises the whole agonising problem – and an increasing problem – of children who are born with some mental or physical defect. You may have to say something in general about this, but you will certainly come across it in your pastoral and counselling work. It is not your business to be an amateur medical adviser, but it is your business to deal with the moral dilemma and the kind of question that the disciples raised with Jesus. Is the answer of Jesus totally valid today? It is valid, I would maintain, but is it totally valid in the light of the increasing knowledge we have of genetics? Is in some cases abortion also a valid answer?

There are occasions, and this may be one of them, when you cannot be dogmatic in your answers, and you may simply have to raise the question and urge compassion.

You do have the duty and the opportunity of dealing with miracle, which you ought to do from time to time. There is not today the difficulty that we faced when I began my ministry, when science was so assured and arrogant in its attitude that it encouraged the notion that anything that couldn't be explained couldn't possibly happen, which is a very unscientific attitude. That is not the outlook of science today. The exceptional and the contingent are today accepted possibilities. That means that miracle is a possibility for science as well as for faith.

The second half of the chapter, dealing with the reaction of the Pharisees and the cross-questioning of the man who had been blind, who is a very real character, throws light on human nature and is worth exploring. By the way, there are occasions, and I think this is one of them, when you may have to preach a sermon in two parts on successive Sundays. If you do so you have to be sure that each part can stand alone, and you ought to do a recapitulation of the first sermon at the beginning of the second. But let the recapitulation be brief, or you will bore those who have already heard the sermon.

I note that on the third and fourth Sundays in Lent you have parables among the suggested lessons. There is the difficult parable of the Fig Tree and the great parable of the Prodigal Son. There are innumerable books on the parables, some which will help and some which will hinder your understanding. I think you ought to know books which deal with parables in general, but you should be chary of books which virtually give you potted sermons on the parables. It is what God is saying to you for your people through a parable that you must preach. Of course, you must be as scrupulous as you can be in your exegesis, but the application of the lesson of the parable must be, as the parables almost always originally were, speaking to the present condition of the congregation.

Don't neglect the parables. We can still teach as Jesus did by parables. Preaching on the parables is not as easy as some people imagine.

The fifth Sunday in Lent – a reference to the three suggested lessons from the Gospels will illustrate the point – is the bridge between Lent and Holy Week which you will be leading your people across. The first of the suggested lessons is about the death and resurrection of Lazarus. It is a lesson which, like our Lord's whole person and ministry, combines the human and the divine. Lazarus is mortally ill. Why did Jesus delay going to help and to heal? This is a question which people will ask you about their own loved ones who are ill. It's a question which, if you bear your people in your heart, you will often ask yourself. And there is no rational answer. But notice, it is a permissible question, and it is a question which implies faith. It is faith that makes the rebuke, 'Lord, if you had been here my brother would not have died' (John 11:21). Was the delay in order that God might be glorified by the miracle of resurrection? Is the picture of the family and friends' party with the risen Lazarus meant to be a foretaste of heaven and the heavenly banquet which is a symbolism used by Jesus? Was it a looking forward in faith and hope to his own death and resurrection, which is God's greatest glory and our greatest assurance of victory over sin and death and the grave?

Those are some of the questions you might ask and try to answer.

The second Gospel lesson on this fifth Sunday is John 12:20-33. It is the account of the Greeks coming to Philip asking to meet Jesus. Philip takes them to Andrew who takes them to Jesus. Andrew only appears actively three times in the Gospels, and, significantly, each time he is introducing someone to Jesus. He is the man who brought others, first his brother Peter, then the lad with the loaves and fish, and here the Greeks. There's a sermon there if you are ever called on to preach to a Caledonian or St Andrew's Society. But it has probably been done by someone before you. There are six possible sermons on the twelve apostles. Choose your own five. The sixth on the fact that the rest are almost all just names – nothing extraordinary about them. The point? Most disciples of Christ are ordinary folk.

The effect of this is to underline for Jesus that his mission to the world is now reaching its climax and that it will be consummated in his death and resurrection. 'I, when I am lifted up from the earth,' he says in this passage, 'will draw all men to myself' (John 12:32).

And, finally, the third lesson, Luke 22:14-30, is from the Last Supper, which we will be looking at more fully in the next chapter on preaching in Holy Week. Here the accent is on the human factor which leads to the cross, the betrayal of the Christ by those nearest to him, on Judas who betrayed him and the rest, who promised to be faithful at all costs but who in the event were to forsake him.

Here, as I say, is the bridge between Lent and Easter. We look forward over that bridge to what is to come, and at the same time we look back to our connection with the Lenten themes which have concerned us, to temptation and repentance and human sin and the forgiveness which is of God's grace and mercy sealed to us in the cross and resurrection.

He died that we might be forgiven,
He died to make us good.

Who of ourselves are no good.

4

HOLY WEEK

I HAVE decided to devote one chapter to preaching through Holy Week.

I do so in the knowledge that at present it is not very common in most of the churches in the United States to have services with a sermon on the days of Holy Week. It is not exceptional in Scotland, but it is not all that common. Most churches will have a service on Good Friday. And several churches of different denominations in a town may unite to have a service each night. In my last parish, St Michael's, Linlithgow, we had during my 18 years there united Holy Week services each evening of Holy Week, except Saturday. And the practice is on the increase not only in Scotland, but, I suspect, also in America. In 1977, after a lecture at St Andrews University to the American School of Theology organised by the late Professor William Barclay, I was given an invitation to conduct Holy Week services in Memphis. There, in addition to a Bible study each morning, we had a service each evening except Saturday. My guess is that before long the observance of Holy Week will be much more wide-spread than it is today. Should this be encouraged? And if so, why?

I think there is a convincing biblical answer to those questions. In the edition I use of the New English Bible, Matthew's Gospel occupies 39 pages. Twelve and a half of those pages are devoted to the eight days from Palm Sunday to Easter. In Mark the proportion is slightly higher. Out of 24 pages, eight and a half are devoted to the events of those days. In Luke's Gospel the proportion, almost one quarter, is the smallest of the four Gospels. It is ten out of 42 pages. And St John's Gospel of 32 pages devotes more than twelve pages to describing what happened from Palm Sunday to Easter. In short, the Gospels, which select the significant events in the life and teaching of Jesus, are agreed in devoting altogether about one third of their space to describing the events of those eight days between Palm Sunday and Easter.

This is not all the biblical evidence that favours encouraging the observance of Holy Week. If we look at the Acts we find that the accent of their preaching falls on the two great and mighty acts: the death and resurrection of Jesus. It is not possible to do the same mathematical analysis of the material in Acts as we have with the Gospels, since they are not chronologically systematic; but the emphasis is, as Peter's sermon puts it: 'God has made him both Lord and Christ, this Jesus whom you crucified' (Acts 2:36). Incidentally, you should not assume that the Gospels are all in chronological order. They are not.

And certainly Paul's letters to the Young Churches, it has been frequently remarked, are very sparse in their account of the teachings and the life of Jesus. There are only two or three paraphrases of Jesus' sayings and not a mention of the virgin birth or the other birth and boyhood stories. But there are abundant and repeated references to the death and resurrection of Jesus and to his continuing presence and power.

It is important to remember that the historical evidence is that the whole idea of observing a Christian Year began with the observance of Easter and what preceded Easter, the crucifixion, and what preceded the crucifixion, the events of the week leading up to it, beginning with Palm Sunday. In other words, it grew up naturally from the biblical emphasis, and this is the emphasis which the Church must maintain if it is to present a balanced and truly Christian faith to the world. And one way of maintaining this – only one way, but one that we should encourage – is a proper observance of Holy Week.

From the beginning of the Christian Church until now, Jerusalem – which was and still is a place of Jewish pilgrimage – has been a place of Christian pilgrimage. When Christians from earliest times went to Jerusalem, they walked in the steps of the Master, and the events of Holy Week were especially imprinted on their minds by visits to the traditional sites of those events.

To this day, and not only on Palm Sunday but every Sunday, pilgrims proceed round the shoulder of the Mount of Olives over the Kidron Valley to the Temple area, waving palm branches and shouting hosannah. It will be recalled that in part of that Temple area our Lord overturned the money exchangers' tables and drove out those who were mingling human profits with God's praise. They will probably recall some of the great parables reputedly spoken on the Tuesday. There may be an excursion arranged to the village of Bethany, to which, on the outskirts of the city, Jesus is reported to have retired each night. They will certainly be taken to the Cenaculum, the traditional site of the large Upper Room where the Last Supper was held on the Thursday, and to Gethsemane, where our Lord agonised while the three disciples slept. And where Judas betrayed him with a kiss. They will see the ruins of the high priest's palace where our Lord was imprisoned and the striated floor of Pilate's guardhouse, where he was mocked by the Roman soldiers. Calvary, they will find, is obscured by so many churches seeking a niche of the hill on which to build that it is no longer a green hill outside the city wall but a horrible witness to the disunity of Christ's Church which he prayed might be one and which, tragically and symbolically, obscures the stark love of God in the cross of Calvary by a squalid elbowing and crowding of each other at what should be the holiest of holy places. There is inevitably some uncertainty about some of the sites. Most of them are traditional, and the site of the resurrection is one of the least certain. There is a traditional site, but many find the site of the garden tomb – the tomb which was discovered by General Gordon – to be a place in which they can more readily find the peace and joy of Easter. Just as many pilgrims find Tiberias – with its everlasting hills and the Sea of Galilee, much as it was in Jesus' day – to be a place where it is easier to imagine Jesus walking and teaching and healing. Cities change, but the hills and the lochs remain.

If you ever have the slightest possibility of visiting the Holy Land, grab it with both hands, for it will drive home to you the truth that Christianity is not a system of ideas, not even a system of theology; it is a series of events, of acts of God, culminating in the act of God which is Christ. It is a happening which happened there and then; and to touch even for a few days that place and feel that his feet trod there, to realise that here he was born, here he lived what he taught, here he died and rose again imperishably alive forever in his Spirit – that quickens the faith. That helps us to realise his reality and renews our worship of him.

It seems to me that that is, in a lesser way, the aim of the observance of Holy Week.

It is to recall each day the events, the happenings, or at least one of the happenings, of each day, to meditate on what is significant about each day.

And, above all, to lead your people to worship as well as to wonder, and to commit themselves again and ever more deeply to him who committed himself for us.

The service each day should at the very beginning recapitulate the events or event of that day. And that should be how the service for Palm Sunday begins, in some such words as these:

This is Palm Sunday.

When the time was come for the Lord Jesus to be received up, he steadfastly set his face to go to Jerusalem. Today we remember his triumphal entry into the Holy City and how he was welcomed with hosannahs and palm-branch waving.

"Blessed is he who comes in the name of the Lord! Hosannah in the highest!"

In *The Worshipbook* you will find suggested lessons and prayers and collects to guide you in preparing your service.

But let me say this in general about preaching in Holy Week. This is a week for emphasising events and for meditation on those events. The proclamation is in letting your people see the act. Here, more than at any other time, the unspoken cry of the people ought to be: 'Sir, we would see Jesus.' And no man or woman should stand between that inarticulate desire and its fulfilment.

We are not given much to meditation, we Presbyterians. We have, to a fault, rationalised our faith. And perhaps this is why we are rather afraid of Holy Week observance, because it is foreign to us. But I would urge you to try. Stick to the mighty acts. Don't adorn them overmuch. Let them speak for themselves. And let the sermon be briefer than usual – 15 rather than 20 minutes! You in any case will probably also find that you will be speaking slower than usual, especially as the week goes on. The pace of meditation is slower than the normal pace of preaching.

If you plan a week's services for Holy Week you will probably find that the sermon will occupy the usual length of time on Palm Sunday, for you will want to use that sermon as an introduction to Holy Week. Making the case for the observance much as I have tried to do in what I have said already. Having posed and answered the question: Why Holy Week? You will then go on to deal with the dramatic happening on the first Palm Sunday.

There is plenty of material to occupy you here and many questions which you could put and, let's hope, with the help of commentaries, try to answer.

There is the instruction to the disciples to procure a donkey, all very secret and mysterious even to the extent of an arranged password: 'The Lord has need of it.' And there are the explanations supplied in Matthew and John that this was done to fulfil the prophecy in Zechariah, that one day a king would come to Jerusalem, in gentleness, riding on a donkey. You may point out that that prophecy was made some five hundred years before they saw its fulfilment in the events of Palm Sunday. It was made at a time when there were attempts at rebuilding Jerusalem, its Temple, and the life of a nation. The Temple had been rebuilt, but the spiritual condition of the nation in those five hundred years had not been restored. They were still seeking someone to lead them, they were looking for a chief to follow and a cause to which they could commit themselves. Our Lord knew the prophecies, and what he arranged on Palm Sunday was an assertion of the claim that in his own person he was the fulfilment of the promise of God foretold by the prophet Zechariah. The people, including the accompanying disciples, recognised that this was what was meant by the manner of his entry into Jerusalem. And later, writing up their account of the occasion, the Evangelists could say, and did say in characteristic phrase: This is that!

You are, of course, familiar with the meaning of the manner of Jesus' coming riding on a donkey. If a king was coming into a territory in war he rode on a war-horse. If he was coming in peace he rode on a donkey. He who is King of Glory is King of Peace.

That was not only implicit in the action of Jesus on Palm Sunday; it was *ex*plicit in the shout of the disciples.

Blessings on him who comes as king in the name of the Lord.

Peace in heaven and glory in the highest.

It is also explicit in the attempt of the Pharisees to silence the disciples and their request to Jesus to stop them. It is also explicit in Jesus' refusal and the words that, according to Luke, he is reported to have spoken in distress over the city so beloved by him and by his people. He wept over it and said, 'Would that even today you knew the things that make for peace! But now they are hid from your eyes' (Luke 19:42).

Is that not a contemporary lament and criticism that still has to be levelled at our civilisation? And the warning that Christ gave on that occasion about the destruction of Jerusalem is only too realistic as a possibility applicable to our world today.

So on this day his disciples and the people hailed him and

welcomed him, but it is clear already that not everyone approved. The act of Jesus was challenged, and ponder the significance of two different attitudes revealed in Matthew's report of what was said by the crowd. There were not only those who acknowledged and rejoiced in the claim implicit in his entry and cried 'Hosanna to the Son of David! Blessed is he who comes in the name of the Lord!' There were also those who asked: 'Who is this?', and who were given the dismissive answer: 'This is the prophet Jesus from Nazareth in Galilee' (Matthew 21:9-11). Prophets were two a penny and Nazareth was a place of no reputation.

This poses the question of Holy Week. The eternal Christ comes to us with his claim, which he does not force on anyone, and he asks us to say who he is. We can reject him outright, as the Pharisees did. We can dismiss him patronisingly as a good man, a man of vision, a prophet who had some homespun truths from which we can still learn something. Or we can wholeheartedly welcome him as the one who comes from God with all the authority of God to show us as individuals and as communities the things that belong to our peace. The Eternal comes to meet our perpetual need for a saviour.

And so to the Monday: 'On this day our Lord returned from Bethany to Jerusalem, cursing the barren fig tree on the way. He cleansed the courts of the Temple and declared that his Father's house should be a house of prayer for all nations.'

The order of that preface follows Mark's Gospel. Matthew and Luke are a little vague about the day of the cleansing of the Temple: they both continue their account after the triumphal entry with the word 'then' and there follows the cleansing of the outer court. But Matthew puts the blasting of the fig tree as happening after the scene in the outer court of the Temple, and introduces that incident with the words 'next morning'. That suggests Matthew almost certainly and Luke possibly thought that the Temple-cleansing event happened shortly after the triumphal entry on Palm Sunday and not on the Monday.

I mention this because it is something that people, if they

read their Bibles intelligently, will notice. There are irreconcilable discrepancies in the Bible, and from time to time you have to point that fact out to your congregation. And it is easier to do it naturally when, as here or in the reporting of the resurrection, accounts of the same event differ in detail. Don't make too much of the fact, but don't gloss it over. You may very well point out that this is of the very stuff of history, and that far from casting doubt on the reliability of an event, those discrepancies add to the historicity of the happening. They had something to tell. It really is of no great moment whether what happened happened on the Sunday or on the Monday. There is nothing strange about a difference over the day or over the sequence of events. You will get that kind of difference among witnesses telling about some exciting event thirty days after the event. The divergence of a day or two after thirty years is neither here nor there, and, if anything, as I say, it emphasises that this happened and shows their very human determination to tell it as they remembered it.

The blasting of the fig tree and the cleansing of the Temple come as a vivid contrast, do they not, to the entry of Jesus into Jerusalem. Here we see him as King of Peace. There we see him exercising his kingship in a decisive and authoritative manner. William Barclay thinks that the story of the fig tree is, without exception, the most difficult story in the gospel. He says that it doesn't ring true. I'm not sure about that. The disciples may have misunderstood what Jesus was looking for when he looked at the fig tree. It's unlikely that Martha and Mary sent him off to Jerusalem without his breakfast. Jesus was a country man. So am I. I could tell, looking at an apple tree in full leaf in my garden in the spring, whether or not it was going to be a good year or a bad year for apples, whether or not there was going to be nothing but leaves. Now I think Professor Barclay, who was not a country man, was right when he says that if we are to make any sense of this incident we must see it as an acted parable. Jesus had come to the very heart of Israel, and at a glance he could see that all that was here was an appearance. This was holy ground, hallowed by the centuries-old faith which had been given to the Israelites as it had been given to no other people. And there was going to be no fruit. Not ever. 'The whole lesson of the incident,' concludes William Barclay, 'is that uselessness invites disaster.' The judgment of God is inevitable, and Christ, who is King of Peace, is also our Judge. He comes in judgment as well as in love.

If you deal with this admittedly difficult passage it might be appropriate to recall the fourth chapter of Jonah, where Jonah sits down in the shade of a castor oil plant, furious that God will not destroy Nineveh. He was glad of the shade. A worm attacks the plant, the leaves flop, and Jonah is exposed to the heat of the sun and wishes he were dead. 'God said to Jonah, "Do you do well to be angry for the plant?" And he said, "I do well to be angry, angry enough to die." And the LORD said, "You pity the plant ... which came into being in a night and perished in a night. And should not I pity Nineveh, that great city, in which there are more than a hundred and twenty thousand persons who do not know their right hand from their left, and also much cattle?"' (Jonah 4:9-11).

And recall, when Jesus saw the city, he wept.

But he was also angry. Whatever way you look at it, and whatever account of the cleansing of the Temple you prefer, it was an angry scene. It was an exercise of his kingly authority, and I believe it is analogous to what happened on the way to the barren fig tree. It was, as Jesus realised, finished. No fruit ever again. On Palm Sunday, Mark tells us, Jesus had a good look around, and I think Mark's order of events makes the most sense. Jesus came that morning to do what he did, and the blasting of the fig tree was the prologue for what was to follow. The fig tree represented Israel.

In retelling the story of the cleansing of the Temple, do not miss the point that it was in the Court of the Gentiles that the buying and selling was going on, the place where non-Jewish inquirers came to learn about the God of Israel. It was the only part of the Temple that they could come into, and Jesus, who came to the world for the world, to gather all of us to God, and who knew that the Jewish faith was a missionary faith, not for Jews only, was hurt and angry when he saw the Gentiles' court cluttered with all the outward show of an ingrown religion that was going through the motions but expected nothing, no fruit, no response, and therefore made no effort, provided no opportunity for others to learn about God. This is the point of Jesus' quotation (partly from Isaiah and partly from Jeremiah): 'Is it not written, "My house shall be called a house of prayer for all the nations?" But you have made it a den of robbers' (Mark 11:17).

This is still his challenge to his Church. We, like the Jews, are so often proud of our Church. We enjoy it and gather to rejoice in the riches of God's grace. But like the robbers who retire to their den to gloat over the riches they have gained, we keep it too much to ourselves. We warm ourselves at the fire of God's love in Christ, but we care not if others are out in the cold.

'The Church,' says Brunner, 'lives by mission as a fire lives by burning.'

The Tuesday of Holy Week by all accounts was a busy day. On this day our Lord spoke the parables of the Two Sons, the Wicked Husbandman, the Marriage Supper, the Ten Virgins, and the Talents. He answered the questioning of the Pharisees, Saduccees, and a certain lawyer. He foretold the destruction of Jerusalem and described the Last Judgment.

Here there is a superabundance of sermon material, an embarrassment of riches. Mark's Gospel gives more than two chapters out of 16 to telling us what was said and done on Tuesday of Holy Week. And the other Evangelists have more to add to what Mark has given us. Most of their additional material is an account of some of the parables of Jesus.

Just as I would hope that on the Monday you would not try to deal with both the blasting of the fig tree and the cleansing of the Temple, so I would not expect you, other than in the preface to your service, to treat all the happenings and sayings of Jesus on this busy day – though the two events can be related.

There are, it seems to me, three courses open to anyone called to preach on this day.

The subject of the sermon might be one incident or one parable selected from the mass of material available. You can easily combine an incident and a parable as, for example, the question put by the chief priests and elders: 'By what authority are you doing these things?' – and the parable about the two sons, the one saying to his father, when given a piece of work to do, that he would get on with the job, then not doing it; and the other refusing, then changing his mind and going ahead. Or you could expound a parable on its own or an incident on its own.

Or the subject of the sermon might be an exposition of one of the extended speeches of Jesus recorded as having been given on this day. For example, the long speech condemning the scribes and the Pharisees in Matthew 23, or the apocalyptic passage in Matthew 24 or Mark 13.

The third choice which I would suggest – and it would be my own personal preference – is to try to summarise the mood of that day and to strike the dominant note which emerges from its happenings, parables, and speeches. As far as possible we should see in this week not a series of separate episodes but how one thing leads to another. We are following the *via crucis*, and the very words that we use – 'way', 'following' – imply movement, a progression from one point to the next.

And it can be demonstrated that the events of the Tuesday follow what happened on the Monday. It all begins significantly with Jesus again in the Temple area and with the question from the lawyers and the Pharisees regarding the authority of Jesus: 'By what authority are you doing these things?' What right had Jesus to enter Jerusalem in that acting-parable way, riding on a donkey? What right had he to condemn the useless fig tree? What right had he to overturn the moneychangers' tables and to expel them from the precincts of the Temple?

There is your connection with what has gone before. Remember that you will not get all the people at every service in Holy Week, and if you can work in a natural recapitulation it is helpful not only to those who are following you day by day as you follow the way to the cross, but also to those who can only get to one or two services.

That forward impetus is the mood of this day. It is a mood of gathering storm and growing conflict, marked at its beginning by the important question of the authority, the right of Jesus to do what he had done and was doing. This is an ongoing question. We still call him Master and Lord, but we still don't do what he says. And remember, judgment does begin at the House of God. But it doesn't end there. The apocalyptic passages make clear that God's judgments are always abroad in the earth, that disobedience by individuals and nations to the light we have, issues in disaster. It is also clear from the hindsight of history that Jesus was referring not only to a Last Judgment in the speeches and parables of this day but also to the destruction of Jerusalem, which took place in AD 70 – within the natural span, but for the cross, of Jesus. But the parables and passages which speak words of warning and rebuke, of judgment and disaster, also speak of the vindication of God and the ultimate triumph of the Son of God. In wrath God remembers mercy and so must we.

In contrast to the busy Tuesday of Holy Week, the next day appears to have been spent by Jesus in the seclusion of Bethany, and the preface to the Wednesday would be to the effect that 'on this day our Lord remained in Bethany, where in the house of Simon the leper a woman anointed him with oil. On this day Judas bargained with the chief priests to betray him'.

For some reason not clear to me, the lectionary in *The Worshipbook* suggests as the lesson from the Gospel, Luke 22:1-16. This is a lesson which begins with the chief priests and others devising some means of getting rid of Jesus. It tells of the decision of Judas to betray him. It then goes on to describe the preparation for the Passover and ends with the beginning of the

Passover meal which took place on the Thursday. This lesson omits the significant account of the anointing by the woman with the ointment. I think a more appropriate lesson would be Matthew 26:1-16, which refers to the main events of the Wednesday without trespassing on what we recognise as the most important event on the Thursday, which is the Last Supper.

The Wednesday is the quiet day which Jesus spent away from the stir and bustle, the excitement, controversy, and crowds in Jerusalem, which was *en fête* preparing for the Passover, that mixture of holiday and Holy Day.

I think this is where, if we are keeping Holy Week, we too should experience a change of mood and help people to make the transition from the excitement and stirring deeds and words of Palm Sunday, the near riot in the Temple courtyard and the stern teaching of Tuesday's parables, to the preparation that Jesus was making for what was to come: the supper, the agony in the garden, the trial, and the cross. There is a slowing of tempo here. This is a day of crisis, but it is a day of few words, though there are enough significant incidents to supply you with material for several sermons.

You might do well to speak to your people on this day, which is a kind of lull before the storm, of the need for quiet in our unquiet world, of the advantage of seclusion, pointing out that this was not only Jesus' practice from time to time (as we learn from the Gospels), but that he also taught what he practised. 'Pray to your Father,' he said, 'in secret', privately, alone (see Matthew 6:6). The growth of interest in Eastern cults in our time, most of which give a greater place to meditation than we are accustomed to doing, may be an indication that we in the Church have not recognised the need for being still and thus knowing God. I came across a surprising quotation from Emerson, showing his appreciation of silence: 'I like the silent church before the service begins better than any preaching.' There is a feeling among some clergy and congregations that there should be a place during almost every service for silent worship.

You will almost certainly at some time want to preach on the lovely incident of the woman with the alabaster flask of ointment. I would ask you to note that even here we have an act of silent devotion by the woman. We have no record that she said anything, not a word. The critics were vocal, but she apparently said nothing. We know from the Gospel what Jesus' interpretation of her act was and his reaction to it. He said that it was a fine thing. He also saw it as a preparation for his funeral. You may also point out that our very consideration of this incident is a fulfilment of our Lord's word of high commendation: 'Wherever this gospel is preached in the whole world, what she has done will be told in memory of her' (Matthew 26:13).

You may feel that there is a dramatic contrast between the action of the woman that day and the action of Judas, but if you do I would urge that the proper tone to adopt when dealing with Judas on this day is neither anger nor condemnation, but rather sad dismay. The next day Judas was to ask: 'Is it I, Lord?' Each of us, as we draw near to the cross, has to ask that fearful question, for it is human sin that brought Jesus to the Cross.

On the next day, Thursday, your preface might be: 'On this day our Lord went again to Jerusalem. In the evening in the Upper Room, he washed the feet of the disciples and instituted the sacrament of his body and blood. He spoke the words of comfort and peace and made the great intercession. In the garden of Gethsemane he endured his agony. Betrayed by Judas and arrested by his enemies, he was taken to prison and to judgment.'

That longish preface for the service for this day gathers together as succinctly as possible the events of a day packed with meaningful happenings and utterances. It is, I believe, important that the preface should give a summary of what happened and that we should be reminded about the preparations for the Passover meal in the Cenaculum, the disciples' refusal to do the service of feetwashing after their walk from Bethany and before the meal, and our Lord's doing the service they were too proud to do. It is right that we should be reminded of some of the con-

versation: our Lord's forecast of betrayal and the disciples' protes-
tations. His words foretelling the cross and his words of reassurance. His prayer for himself and for them and for us – always, he
intercedes for us. The action after supper of breaking the bread
and giving it and the cup to them: 'This is my body ... this is my
blood ... Do this in remembrance of me.' Then the going out in
the night down the hill to Gethsemane, his agonising prayer while
the disciples fall asleep. The betrayal by Judas and the arrest.

You may feel that the wealth of material here is bewildering,
and you will realise that if you are to preach on an event or utterance of this day you will have to be strictly selective.

It is possible to do what the writers of the Gospels did for us.
They selected what especially appealed to them in all the happenings of this day. You may do the same by taking the events
of the day as recorded by Mark, another year as in Matthew,
another year as in Luke, and a fourth as in John, simply adding
a brief meditation or comment on what is said and done.

But I imagine you will be inclined to concentrate on one of
three events which I believe are most significant. I mention them
not in order of importance, but in the order of their occurrence.
The three are: the washing of the disciples' feet; the institution
of the Lord's Supper; and the agony in the garden of Gethsemane. The central significance of those three events is that they
indicate that Jesus chose the way of the cross. If in Holy Week we
show how what his enemies and friends did or failed to do made
the cross inevitable, we must emphasise that Jesus, while he shrank
from the cross, at the same time submitted to it and accepted it.
The opening words of the institution of the Supper as given by
St Paul are of the utmost importance for our understanding not
just of this day but of the gospel. It was 'on the night when he was
betrayed' that our Lord took the bread and broke it and gave it
and said, 'This is my body' (I Corinthians 11:23-24). Before men
had done their worst to him our Lord did his best for us. Before he
was taken he gave himself. This is the prevenient grace of God in
Christ. That is the gospel, the amazing good news of this day.

And so to Good Friday, which deserves the adjective precisely because we see it in the context of the night before and of what is to come after on Easter morning. It is what has gone before and what we know is to come after that allow us to survey the wondrous cross on which the Prince of Glory died and to follow the events of this day summarised in the preface: 'On this day our Lord was tried before the high priests, then by Pilate, thereafter by Herod, and then by Pilate again, was scourged, mocked, and condemned to death. He was led out to Calvary. At nine o'clock he was crucified. At intervals he spoke the Seven Words from the Cross. At three o'clock he bowed his head and died.'

Who is sufficient for those things and to preach on those things? The cross silences us all with a deathly hush. Here as we are compelled to look at the cross we must feel in the words of Paul: 'O the depth!' (see Romans 11:33). People are almost overwhelmed by the enormity of the mystery of the cross, and never more so than on Good Friday. One thing that is not appropriate to this day is to treat people to your own or anybody else's theory of atonement. We are not saved by a theology of atonement, we are saved by the act of God in Christ, who in the cross makes known his love for us in that while we were yet sinners Christ died for us. That is the message of the cross this day.

And it is a message which is demonstrated in the variety of persons and types whom we see contributing to the crucifixion. The sinners whose varied sins brought the Christ to the cross have many faces. There are the establishment figures represented by the secular leaders, the lawyers, and the scribes. There are the religious leaders represented by the Pharisees and the chief priests. There are the political leaders represented by Pilate and Herod; and there are those who only obeyed orders, the Roman soldiers who mocked him with a crown of thorns. There was the crowd who were so easily misled and who chose Barabbas, the violent man, in preference to Jesus because they did not know, as he had said earlier that week, 'the things that make for peace' (Luke 19:42). And there were those who had been closest to him:

Judas who betrayed him, Peter who denied him, and the others who were afraid and who forsook him and fled.

When we hear on Good Friday the question in the black spiritual, 'Were you there when they crucified my Lord?', and when we look at those who were there, we see ourselves in them. We see our humanity in its sin and folly. We see in the darkness of that hour that we love darkness rather than light because our deeds are evil. And evil deeds, and the crucial evil deed of the cross, are not crass, gross and obvious evil. They are the common evil of common humanity. The refusal of the Establishment, secular, political, and religious, to accept the challenge of Christ to be renewed, to be radically reformed. The refusal of the mass of us to think for ourselves and make right choices. The refusal to stand up and be counted among the friends of Christ because we are afraid. Yes, we were there when they crucified the Lord.

But we cannot leave it at that. It is not the end of the story, not even the end of the story on Good Friday. We must recapitulate and remind people of Maundy Thursday and of his self-giving while he was being betrayed. The cross is not just our own hideous doing and horrible in our sight. It is God's doing and wondrous in our eyes because of that prevenient act. The word of the cross is Christ's word addressed to God on behalf of all of us sinners: 'Father, forgive them; for they know not what they do' (Luke 23:34).

I have known, in my own church very occasionally and in other churches more commonly, a three-hour vigil kept on Good Friday in commemoration of our Lord's three hours of darkness on the cross. The proper theme of such a meditation is the Seven Words from the Cross. I see no special merit in observing this at the precise hours recorded in the Gospel, noon to three in the afternoon. What I would like to see is a three-hour service on the theme of the Seven Words from the Cross which would be thoroughly ecumenical, seven twenty-minute services with a five-minute silence between each service for meditation and for people to come or to go or to stay for one or more of the services within the three-hour vigil. By ecumenical I mean that the service would be planned together by a Presbyterian, a Roman Catholic, a Baptist, a Congregational, a Methodist, a Reformed, an Episcopal – alas, we have many more than seven varieties of denomination to choose from – but there you have seven, and in many towns and cities it should be possible, sometime, somewhere, to have such a service of united witness and worship of him who prayed that we might be one. It is, of course, not impossible to share such a service with fewer than six of your fellow ministers – for example, two of like mind could carry through such a service, and it is not beyond the capacity of one man or woman to conduct such a service – but if you do I would recommend you to enlist the services of seven of your congregation to read the appropriate lessons containing the Seven Words.

A final word: let me emphasise again that you should keep to the acts and words of Jesus as far as possible to the appropriate day on the various days of Holy Week. Not only is there sufficient variety in the happenings and utterances of each day to help you lead your people, but you will find, as you read again and think of those things, your insight into the meaning of the events of Holy Week is constantly refreshed and deepened. I hope you will find, as I have found, that at this time people will want to follow in the footsteps of Christ coming over the shoulder of the Mount of Olives on Palm Sunday and to hear again the shouts of hosannah, to watch the cleansing of the Temple and listen to its lesson, to hear the great familiar parables, and in Bethany to join in spirit in the quiet of the spectacular devotion of an unknown woman, to recall the institution of the sacrament of holy communion on the night on which he was betrayed, and to watch and identify themselves with those who crucified him on Good Friday, and to appreciate something of the meaning of his penultimate word: 'It is finished' (John 19:30). This is the culmination. The last thing that Jesus could do for us was to die for us. But it is not the last thing that God can do.

5

THE EASTER CYCLE

ONE of the arguments for observing Holy Week is simply that it helps us more fully to understand what Easter meant to the disciples and the first followers of Jesus. If we have not entered into their experience and their feelings, in imagination at least, during the week which began in apparent triumph on Palm Sunday and ended with the utter disaster of the cross on the Friday and their dead leader buried in a borrowed tomb, how can we enter into the experience of Easter and what that meant to them? If we have not identified with them in their sin and shame and despair, we cannot readily enter into the transformation in them which Easter effected and share their renewed faith and hope and love for the living God who brought the Lord Jesus again from the dead.

The Easter cycle, which begins with Easter Day, continues for the forty days that, according to the New Testament, the risen Lord remained with his disciples before he parted from them at the Ascension. It was natural that the Church which followed the events and appearances of Jesus during those forty days and pondered their meaning should take into consideration in the same period the fact of the Ascension and the meaning for faith of that event. Since the normal day for the Church to meet for worship was the Sunday, you have the five Sundays after Easter and before the Ascension (which always falls on a weekday), *plus* the Sunday after Ascension, making a 50 day period of seven Sundays devoted to the resurrection, its meaning and consequences, including the significant inevitability of Ascension.

What should one preach during this period? How should one plan one's sermons? In one sense the answers are simple: you preach the resurrection, and at least for the first three Sundays there is much to be said for following events as recorded in the Gospels.

1   On the first Sunday, Easter Day, you would take your text and theme from the record of Easter morning according to Luke or Mark or John. And I see no reason why in the fourth year you should not consider the event according to the record in Matthew.

2   On the second Sunday you will find ample and dramatic material in the account of what happened 'eight days later' in the appearance to Thomas recorded by John 20:26-29; or in the post-Easter rumour reported in Matthew 28:11-15; or in the appendix to Mark. I prefer these lessons to the lesson from John 21 which is suggested by *The Worshipbook* for this Sunday in the third year. I think that lesson properly belongs not to the week after Easter but, as the Gospel says, 'after these things' (John 21:1, KJV) – *ie* some time later. I would be inclined to deal with it on the third Sunday after Easter.

3   On the third Sunday then, as I suggest, you have the appearance in Galilee, and I would take John 21:1-14 one year, and the challenge to Peter in John 21:14-25 another year. And, though it is out of sequence, you should preach sometime, and more than once, on the lesson of the lovely Emmaus story that happened on Easter afternoon and evening. It can fit in on the third Sunday, as can the second part of Luke 24, which has one of the inspired texts to be found in the New English Bible in verse 41, where we read of the disciples: 'They were still unconvinced, still wondering, for it seemed too good to be true.'

There is your raw material, the record of the resurrection in the Gospels. But what are you to make of it? Joseph Gelineau quotes in a recent book, *The Liturgy Today and Tomorrow* (New York: Paulist Press), from a poll of French Roman Catholics, that only one in three believes in the resurrection. Would the proportion be any higher among Protestants? I think it would take a very bold person to maintain that it was, and if that is the situation we have to face it. But how? Not by dogmatism for its own sake.

We should recognise two things here. The first is that there are many who don't believe in the resurrection and who feel guilty about their unbelief. The second is that the unbelief of many is not so much because it is a difficult thing to believe as because they don't see the point of the resurrection.

It is our task to help them through doubt to faith and through faith to understanding.

It should help them to realise that doubt is no reason to feel guilty; nor, for that matter, a reason for feeling boldly modern.

When on Easter morning the women went to the tomb, they had no doubts about the purpose of their visit. They were going to prepare a dead body. They were going to do the last rites. They had no thought of resurrection.

When they came and told the disciples, *they* had no doubts. They were quite sure that the women were talking nonsense. Luke, you remember, was a doctor, and you find that he occasionally, quite unconsciously, employs medical terms. The word translated as 'an idle tale' (Luke 24:11 RSV) or 'nonsense' (NEB) is the same word in Greek from which we get the English word *delirium.* They thought the women were raving, and they said so.

It is quite clear that no one expected the resurrection. But on Easter morning before daybreak, both the friends and the enemies of Jesus were finally convinced that the grave was empty. Is it not to the credit of the writers of the Gospels that they frankly admit that everyone was surprised by the event and slow to accept the possibility of resurrection? One other point: the fact that Matthew, Mark, Luke, and John give differences of detail regarding precisely what was seen and who saw what on Easter Day, to me adds to the credibility of the central startling event. That is what I would expect from witnesses of such an astonishing happening. If they all agreed in detail, one might suspect that that was the story they had agreed to tell.

The only explanation other than resurrection suggested by Jesus' enemies as to what happened is recorded by Matthew, who says that the elders and chief priests bribed the soldiers who came to tell them that the grave was empty and instructed them to say that 'his disciples came by night and stole him away' while the soldiers were asleep. That is a very feeble explanation. For one thing the disciples were in no condition to attempt such an escapade. They were frightened, and they were in utter despair. For another, if soldiers sleep on watch they don't come and tell the authorities. And in any case, if they slept on duty how could they see anything! The explanation is incredible.

But I think it is comforting to the doubter in all of us to realise that the first reaction of the witnesses to the resurrection was disbelief. And this should be given a mention on Easter Day, but perhaps simply a mention, so that people can relate with the first witnesses. You have an opportunity of dealing *in extenso* with doubt on the second Sunday, when you have Thomas's response to the secondhand reporting of the fact that Jesus was alive, and Jesus' appearance to Thomas and his challenge, Thomas's confession, and Jesus' response. Remember, we are those who have not seen and yet may have this blessed faith that Christ is alive and always with us.

Some of your time in the Sundays that follow Easter may legitimately be taken up in dealing with doubts about the resurrection; and in speculation about with what body Jesus rose. People do wonder about that, and the New Testament evidence is ambiguous. On the one hand, they didn't always immediately recognise him. Mary thought he was a gardener, the couple on the Emmaus Road said he must be a stranger, and the disciples were afraid he was an apparition when he first appeared. On the other hand, Mary did recognise him when he spoke to her – though she was forbidden to touch him. The couple recognised him at Emmaus when he broke bread with them. He reassured the disciples that he was not a ghost but flesh and blood, and he challenged them, and later Thomas, to examine the stigmata. I think all we can say is that it was Jesus who rose from the dead and appeared, but it was Jesus with a difference, and the *difference* is not surprising. And we do well to leave it at that.

There is then not a hope in many of us that, by the forgiveness which Jesus has won for us, we too may be different when we rise from death. The joy of Easter is the fact of resurrection, not the facts about resurrection. And if our people are going to enter into that joy we have to help them to see the meaning of the fact of resurrection and to appreciate how important the event of Easter is for the Christian faith. It is not too much to say that without the fact of resurrection there would be no Christian faith.

Consider the situation of the disciples at the time of and after the crucifixion. They had played an ignoble part. Judas had betrayed Jesus and committed suicide. Peter had denied him and wept tears of shame. They all forsook him and fled. The picture we have of them after the crucifixion is of men demoralised and despairing, huddled together behind locked doors in near panic. Those are not the men who could conceivably go out with great courage to tell the world, beginning where they were, that Jesus of Nazareth who had been crucified had risen from the dead, was alive, and was, by this act of God, vindicated as the Son of God and the Saviour of the world unless they were sure it was true, unless the resurrection was for them the fact ultimately beyond all doubt. Note that even after the first appearances of Jesus, they didn't know what to do. 'I am going fishing,' said Peter; and they said, 'We will go with you'. Back to the fishing, back to nothing-ality! (Jeremiah 21). There's a sermon for you.

The transformation of the disciples from the frightened, defeated men they were to the confident, faith-full men they became is part of the inescapable evidence for the truth of the resurrection. There is no other plausible explanation for the evident change in them, and for the existence of the Christian Church in all the world, continuing to this day because of the faith that Jesus Christ both died and rose again and is alive forever. 'After two thousand years,' writes Hans Kung in *On Being a Christian* (Garden City, NY: Doubleday), p 463 ...

> *Jesus of Nazareth still lives for mankind. What has kept him alive? Who testified to him time after time before mankind? Would he have remained alive, merely living on in a book? Did he not remain alive because he lived for two thousand years in the minds and hearts of innumerable human beings? .... Without this community of people who have committed themselves to his cause, Jesus would not have remained alive in mankind. And, without it, that little book* [the New Testament] *would never have existed in which the oldest and best records of him are collected.*

True, but he continued to live, and his story was told and recorded because he first rose from the dead and came back alive to meet with his disciples, to demonstrate, not that death was cancelled, but that death was conquered.

So far in discussing the Eastertide theme I have directed your attention to the record of Christ's post-crucifixion appearances in the Gospels, but you will also find rich material for your preaching in the book of Acts and in Paul's epistles.

The book of Acts begins with a synopsis of the appearances of Jesus over forty days. In Acts 2 you should note that in the first Christian sermon preached by Peter on the day of Pentecost the most prominent place is given to the resurrection. And that this was a dominant emphasis in Peter's preaching is evident from Acts 10:36-41, where he recounts the main gospel facts: 'You know ... how God anointed Jesus of Nazareth with the

Holy Spirit and with power' – a reference to Jesus' baptism – 'how he went about doing good and healing all who were oppressed by the devil, for God was with him. And we are witnesses to all that he did both in the country of the Jews and in Jerusalem. They put him to death by hanging him on a tree; but God raised him on the third day and made him manifest; not to all people but to us who were chosen by God as witnesses, who ate and drank with him after he rose from the dead.'

Notice that both the Gospels and Acts are strong not on systematic theology, but on rehearsing the mighty acts. I believe this is important, and perhaps especially important in a day when, through ill-digested biblical criticism, demythologizing, and modern scholarship applied rigorously to the New Testament, the notion has got about that the basic facts of Christ are all uncertain. This is not so. The New Testament comes out of all the devoted research that has been done and is still being done with the substance of the main facts as firm as they possibly can be. People need to be told that and to be reminded of what the facts are.

But they also need to understand the meaning of the facts, and you will find no better guide than the first theologian of the Church, the Apostle Paul. And, as you might expect, Paul is the great theologian of the resurrection. I would, however, advise you to preach from Colossians 3 or from I Corinthians 15, not on the first Sunday, not on Easter Day – though the lectionary suggests these as lessons for Easter Day – but on one of the subsequent Sundays. I would also keep the great Easter doxology in I Peter – the other epistle suggested for Easter Day – as a doxology. The doxologies are shouts of praise and don't readily lend themselves to sermonic analysis.

But take I Corinthians 15, and a few verses earlier than verse 20, which is where the lectionary suggests you begin. Begin at verse 14, where Paul looks at the deep meaning of Easter, and he does it by asking them to suppose that Christ was not raised: suppose there was no resurrection, what then? 'If Christ has not been raised, then our preaching is in vain and your faith is in vain,' and then follows not only your text but a synopsis for your sermon: 'If Christ has not been raised, your faith is futile and you are still in your sins. Then those ... who have fallen asleep in Christ have perished' (I Corinthians 15:14, 17-18). There you have spelled out:

- The consequence for faith in God – if no resurrection;
- The consequence for us – if no resurrection;
- The consequence for a life to come – if no resurrection.

The consequence for faith in God is that faith is emptied of its content. And you can see how that is so. It logically follows. If God is love as Jesus taught, and he allowed the cross, and the cross is the end of Jesus, then, at the very least, God cannot be the Lord God Almighty.

If God is the Lord God Almighty and allowed the cross, and the cross is the end of Jesus, then, at the very least, he cannot be love. There is a divine inevitability about resurrection.

And the consequence for us if there is no resurrection? We are still in our old state of sin. It is back to that normality, no hope.

And you can see how that is so. As we saw so clearly in Holy Week, the cross is the starkest demonstration of our own sinfulness. In the cross Jesus took upon himself the full weight of sinful humanity. He was made sin, Paul is bold enough to say, but he was made sin for a saving purpose. He gave himself to save the world and to break the force of sin, and if the cross is the end then Jesus' bid to be our Saviour from sin and to hold out the hope of forgiveness and continued renewal fails. Sin is conqueror, not Christ. Hence it follows that you and I are still in our old state of sin. Nothing has changed. If he did not rise we cannot rise with him to new life.

And the third consequence? What hope of a life to come if the one who believed in God's power over life and death, if the one who was the nearest ever on earth to God, never got through death, if for him death was the final dead end of life, what hope have we in a life to come? 'Then those ... who have fallen asleep in Christ' – those who have died believing in him, says Paul with brutal frankness – 'have perished.' Lost. Gone – not gone before, but gone forever.

The dire consequences of no resurrection are no grounds for believing in the resurrection, but they are every reason for thinking seriously about what we are doing if we allow people lightly to dismiss the resurrection as a meaningless and unnecessary superstition. It is literally vital for faith in God, for deliverance from the human condition by the grace of God, and for any hope for any life to come.

In this passage Paul goes from the stark contemplation of the dire consequences of no resurrection, from that nightmare, to the great affirmation, 'But in fact Christ has been raised from the dead' (I Corinthians 15:20), and he goes on to spell out what that means. Christ is the first fruits of the mighty harvest of the dead. The man Christ Jesus, the second Adam, comes to rescue the fallen first Adam and all his sinful heirs. 'For as in Adam all die, so also in Christ shall all be made alive' (I Corinthians 15:22). And at the end of the day God will be vindicated, and his reign established.

Only the cross and the resurrection together make the gospel.

The theme of immortality, you will not be surprised to notice, is suggested by several of the lessons, particularly from the epistles of Peter and John and the book of Revelation, as a proper theme for this season, and so it is. It is not a theme which you may find has a strong appeal to you when you are young. In part that is because we have too easily accepted the criticism of the gospel as 'pie in the sky when you die', and we want to counter that by a greater attention to the relevance of the gospel to the here and now. In part also we are inclined to think of eternal life as something which (we hope) happens when we die, and when we are young we are not ready to die just yet. But you must remember that however important the here and now is

– and it was important to Jesus, so important that in his parables he suggests that what we do here and now determines what happens to us there and then – the here and now is only a fraction of our life. And eternal life in the teaching of Jesus is the future present, it begins here and now and continues there and then. Also you are faced and your people are faced continuously with the fact of death, and you must hold out to them the Christian hope of immortality. You will, I trust, avoid what Niebuhr describes as an undue 'curiosity about the furniture of heaven or the temperature of hell', but, with all the authority of the gospel, you will speak of both, for, in a phrase of my old teacher Professor G T Thomson, translator of Barth's earliest work, 'A heaven without a hell is not worth a damn'.

Later I will have something more to say about preaching the Christian hope in the context of All Saints' and In Memoriam services and sermons, but you would do well, before such direct occasions come upon you and your congregation, to prepare them and to lay the groundwork of sound teaching on eternal life; and a short series, say of three sermons, giving the New Testament, post-Easter teaching of Christian faith on this important subject, which too often is neglected in our preaching, would come naturally in the second half of Eastertide.

The first of such a series might be on 'The Hope of Immortality', and the text might be I Corinthians 15:19.

Down through the ages many have pondered the mystery of death. In part we are burdened and in part fascinated by the fact of death. On the edge of my last parish in Scotland there was excavated one of the most ancient burial grounds ever to be discovered in Scotland. It was dated some 3000 years before the birth of Christ and belonged in part to what was called the beaker people. A beaker is a drinking vessel, a tankard made of clay: among the remains found at this burial ground were also found the shards of those beakers, hence the name, the beaker people. This is very ancient evidence of something that is almost universal, the burying of the dead with provision of food and drink for them in some kind of life beyond the grave. This practice is found in places and among people as far apart as the ancient Egyptians and the ancient Greeks, among Pictish Scots and primitive Africans and American Indians. The practice of spiritualism is a more sophisticated expression of this almost universal hope of immortality.

It has to be recognised that this hope does not originate with the Bible. It is older and more widespread. The Old Testament, by and large, supports it, mainly by accepting it and taking it for granted. One can instance David's comment on the death of his child born of Bathsheba: 'I shall go to him, but he will not return to me' (II Samuel 12:23). But notice, this assumption of survival is not particularly Christian. To say that this life is not the end is not saying anything specifically Christian. Survival is one thing. Immortality is another. Immortality is something which is given or withheld. Survival may be natural. Immortality is supernatural. This mortal must put on immortality.

The purpose of survival, according to the New Testament, is for judgment, and notice in the New Testament mercy is always part of judgment. On God's judgment and mercy depend whether or not we receive immortality. If we are in Christ, with all that that means, we rise with him to the life immortal. If we are not, we are lost, we are perished and perishable. That is the significance of the symbolism of the fires of hell.

The second sermon might be on 'The Conditions of Immortality'. After a recapitulation of where you had arrived in your first sermon, you might embark on an examination of any one of the judgment parables, eg the parable of the Sheep and the Goats in Matthew 25:31-46.

This parable and other parables and sayings of Jesus have this in common: they teach that we survive death for the purpose of receiving what is coming to us, and what is to come is an alternative, an either/or. The Bible has different terms in different places to describe the alternative. It is either heaven or hell, eternal life or eternal death, sometimes called the second death. It is either immortality or damnation, and what is of prime importance is to try to see the grounds on which God makes his judgment and destines us to one or the other.

The first thing that has to be said is this: the very fact that there is an alternative at all is due to the work of Jesus Christ. Our faith is that Jesus Christ has opened the kingdom of heaven to all believers. Not one of us on our own can storm heaven. It is only by the grace of God that we win safe home at last. Because we belong to the human race, the fallen race, humanly speaking we have no alternatives but death and survival after death for condemnation. We are doomed to die. That's what the Bible means by quaint statements like, 'as in Adam all die, so also in Christ shall all be made alive' (I Corinthians 15:21), or 'Christ Jesus … brought life and immortality to light' (II Timothy 1:10), or Jesus' own claim: 'I came that they may have life, and have it abundantly' (John 10:10).

Jesus came to do for us what we cannot do for ourselves, to cancel out the disqualification of sin, to pay the price of sin which is death, even death on a cross, that we might have the alternative of immortality. His resurrection and return is the proof above all proofs that he has conquered death for everyone and has opened the kingdom of heaven to all believers.

You may want to touch upon the question of what about those who have not heard about Jesus. We cannot be dogmatic here, but if we behold the glory of God in the face of Jesus Christ we see a God who was infinitely compassionate to the unorthodox and the outsider, and I don't believe that God will shut out from heaven those who could not know him of whom they had not heard.

The important thing for those who have heard of Jesus Christ and his bursting of the gates of hell, and his call to us here and now to seek first his kingdom is our response. Note that some versions of the Apostles Creed correctly read for 'hell' the 'place of the dead'.

Field Marshal Montgomery, on the Sunday after VE Day,

came to the unit to which I was attached and addressed the men. On that occasion, after expressing thanks to God for the victory which had been obtained at the cost of much sacrifice, Montgomery said something like this: 'Remember that victory gives us an opportunity – an opportunity for a fuller and a better life – it is no guarantee that the opportunity will be grasped. That depends on us.' Obviously true. That victory provided an alternative to the hell of subjugation to Germany and the spirit which had possessed Germany. It was and it is no guarantee that we will grasp the opportunity. It is similar with the blood and sacrifice and the costly victory of Christ. By what he has done he has presented us with an alternative and opportunity, a way of escape, but how shall we escape if we neglect so great a salvation?

The answer to the terrified jailer's question, 'What must I do to be saved?' is still 'Believe in the Lord Jesus, and you will be saved' (Acts 16:30-31).

But here we come to an apparent division to be found in the New Testament, in the history of the Church, and one you commonly see and hear among people today.

On the one hand you have a grand evangelical word from the Gospel: 'God so loved the world, that he gave his only begotten Son, that whosoever believeth in him should not perish, but have everlasting life' (John 3:16, KJV). There the emphasis is on, and the condition is, faith.

On the other hand you have the judgment parable of the Sheep and the Goats, in which the judgment depends on what those to be judged have done or failed to do. In other words, here, apparently, the emphasis is on and the condition is works.

In Paul you have the famous statement, 'by grace are ye saved through faith ... *not* of works, lest any man should boast' (Ephesians 2:8-9 KJV, emphasis added). And in the letter of James you have an equally well-known saying: 'What does it profit ... if a man says he has faith but has not works? Can his faith save him? ... faith apart from works is dead' (James 2:14, 26). And it is not sufficient to dismiss James' letter, as Luther did, as 'an epistle of straw'. Both positions can be defended on biblical grounds, but you want to look at what is said very closely; and if you do you will find that this division is more apparent than real. The parable of the Sheep and the Goats, for example, makes clear that what was done by those commended was done by them because they discerned Christ, they had received his revelation, they were the twice born who were so humble that they didn't know that they were serving him. While those who were condemned for what they omitted to do were condemned because they had not walked and acted in the light of Christ. And significantly, they too did not know. Ponder the common agnosticism of those who did and won heaven and those who did not and were condemned. (NB: Luke 7:1-10 also.)

Ultimately it is nothing in us, nothing of ourselves which is immortal. It is the Spirit that is given in Christ through faith in him that saves us. That is the immortal fact, and the Spirit has always a practical and material expression. Christ in us is the hope of glory. And if we have that Spirit and walk with him, we will show that Spirit and that we belong to his fellowship, in the life we live and the words we speak and the deeds we do We will be trusting always in his forgiveness, never presuming yet always hoping in his mercy when we fail, and for his strength to be made perfect in our weakness.

The third sermon might be entitled 'The Place of Immortality'. Again, after briefly covering the ground over which you have been travelling, you will now take up a theme which at one and the same time baffles and intrigues us. What will life after death be like, and where will we spend eternity? Incidentally, I think you will find that people are more curious about heaven than they are about hell. One is tempted to speculate that this is because of our hope of heaven and our fear of hell. But that is more speculation – both are beyond our ken.

One of the most difficult problems in speaking of immortality, eternity, heaven, and hell is that obviously immortality and heaven in a very real sense are beyond our experience. But not only that, the only experience we have and the only terms we can employ are earthly experience and earthly terms in talking about them. Time, for example, is an earthly concept, determined and measured by the movement of the earth in relation to the solar system. Eternity is not just an extension of time, and it is a mind-boggling idea to think of a life which is eternal and which is not measured by and conditioned by time, which is not a time continuum. Similarly, a place is pinpointed in relation to other places. It is identified by its position on a map, by its longitude and latitude. We recognise a place by its scenery. It is almost impossible to think of a place as a place if it is not a place in that recognisable sense. Again, place is an earthly concept which is not appropriate to heaven which is otherworldly. This is very difficult, and I need hardly advise you not to embark too far on the voyage of discovery, because you'll get sunk and your people will get lost trying to think of heaven, which is in the future for them (we hope), but which to talk of as 'future' or 'after' death is inappropriate, because 'future' and 'after' are time terms, and heaven is beyond time. And I'm not sure but that 'beyond' is not itself a time term. It really is impossible, as I have said, to think of heaven which is not a place.

Perhaps positively you can point out that immortality, eternal life according to the New Testament, is something that begins now. It is on our faith expressed in our living that by God's mercy we have eternal life beginning now. Is this not what is meant by being 'born again' (a meaningful phrase used very sparingly in the New Testament)? It is that life which goes on with the life to come.

And as to the place, you will have to interpret for your people all that the book of Revelation with its picture of heaven is saying. That is a very Eastern book full of Eastern promise in Eastern terms. All that about the gates of pearl and the golden pavements and the hallelujah chorus that the book of Revelation is saying is: 'Heap all the riches and splendour of this earth together, gather all that is most precious and exceedingly magnificent, and the half has not been told you.' It is a vision. It is imagining beyond all our imagination. Paul said this when he said, 'Eye hath not seen, nor ear heard, neither have entered into the heart of man, the things which God hath prepared for them that love him' (I Corinthians 2:9, KJV). You should be aware of the truth in Rupert Brooke's poem 'Heaven':

Fish say, they have their Stream and Pond;
But is there anything Beyond?
... ...
One may not doubt that, somehow, Good
Shall come of Water and of Mud,
And sure, the reverent eye must see
A Purpose in Liquidity.
... ...
Oh! never fly conceals a hook,
Fish say, in the Eternal Brook,
But more than mundane weeds are there,
And mud, celestially fair;
... ...
Unfading moths, immortal flies,
And the worm that never dies,
And in that Heaven of all their wish,
There shall be no more land, say fish.

Two things in particular we still ask ourselves, and you will be asked, God help you. One is, 'What will heaven be like?' and the other, 'Will we meet again with those we have loved?' We have to try to answer those questions remembering the limitations of our knowledge that I have already touched on.

Personally, I find the most helpful picture is, as so often, Jesus' picture of heaven. It is quite different from the picture in Revelation. You find it in the passage which, I suggest, might be your text for this sermon: John 14:1-4. The phrase he uses to describe heaven is 'my Father's house'. Heaven is God's home, where God is. 'I go to prepare a place for you,' said Jesus, ' ... that where I am you may be also' (John 14:3). We are going home to God.

And the answer to the second part of the question, 'Will we meet again with those we have loved?' is implicit in that picture. Home is a place of fellowship, of community. It is where family and friends gather. Jesus is not very explicit about recognising one another in heaven, and I believe he is not explicit because the possibility of not meeting with and recognising those we have loved in the world to come never occurred to him.

Harry Lauder, a Scottish singer and comedian, had a favourite song which he wrote after the death of his wife, and which was very popular with audiences all over the world because it struck a chord and expressed a firm hope implanted in the hearts of men and women of all nations:

Keep right on to the end of the road,
Keep right on to the end.
Though the way be long
Let your heart be strong,
Keep right on round the bend.
Though you're tired and weary
Still journey on
Till you come to that happy abode
Where all you love
And are thinking of
Will be there
At the end of the road.

There is much about heaven that is beyond our knowledge, but it is a great thing to be able with all the authority of Jesus to picture heaven as the home of the God and Father of our Lord Jesus Christ, where he is and where, by his mercy, we may be also.

The Ascension, according to the New Testament, took place

forty days after Easter, and the Sunday after Ascension ends the Easter section of the Christian Year.

It is a logical ending, almost as inevitable as gravity. What goes up must come down. He who came down, and went down to the grave, and rose again from the dead, had to go back where he came from. He came out of mystery into history, and he goes back into mystery. He comes from God, he goes back to God. Is that too vague?

Well, let us look at the possibilities after resurrection. There are three.

The first and obvious one would be that Jesus by the power of God having conquered death would just die. That would be a bit of an anticlimax, and I have never heard it put forward as a serious suggestion. It would be a denial of his true divinity.

The second would be that he lived on, a kind of Peter Pan, always there but never growing old. That is equally repugnant as an alternative. It would be a denial of his true humanity.

The third possibility is the biblical one. And notice how matter-of-fact the Bible is in telling us what happened. There is nothing psychedelic about their account. There are no flashing lights, no thunder rolls reverberating around the hills. There is no dramatic lift-off. Their description of what happened is prosaic because it seemed to them the proper conclusion to the life, death, and resurrection of Jesus, that he should lead them out, bless them, and, in Luke's words, 'while he blessed them' be parted from them.

They accepted the Ascension and, significantly, they returned to Jerusalem with great joy and spent all their time in the Temple area praising God. One of the most significant things about the Ascension is that there is not the slightest suggestion of loss. Paradoxically, they are aware that Jesus has gone to be with them always. 'Let us go fishing, we've had it.' There is not a hint of that attitude in their action.

You will find, I think, that people are inclined to accept the Ascension as the disciples did, but only if, like the disciples, they believe in the resurrection. Perhaps that is why there is so little comment and questioning regarding the Ascension compared with the considerable doubt and questioning which you will have to deal with regarding the resurrection.

But, remembering the place given to the Ascension, however laconically, in the Gospels and in Acts and the epistles, and remembering its mention in that briefest of the classical creeds, the Apostles' Creed – he 'ascended to heaven, [and] sits at the right hand of God' – you may feel that you are called to preach on it sometime.

I would expect you to be as laconic about the fact and the mechanics of the Ascension as the New Testament writers are. You would be advised to address yourself to the question: What is the significance of Ascension? What does Mark's Gospel mean, for example, when near the end it states: 'The Lord Jesus … was taken up into heaven, and sat down at the right hand of God?'

You might well consider it appropriate to indicate that here clearly Mark is using the only terms we have, terms of space and time, to describe what happened. It was 'after he had spoken to them' that 'the Lord Jesus … was taken up'. This implies, as is popularly accepted, that heaven is a place that in relation to earth is 'up', and this kind of terminology is not to be scoffed at, so long as we recognise that it is an earthly term for a heavenly condition.

Similarly, it is wise to point out that there is an anthropomorphic metaphor employed in saying that Jesus took his seat at the right hand of God. The heavenly Jesus hasn't got a seat, nor has God a right hand. But a good metaphor is a meaningful metaphor, and the expression 'seated at the right hand of God' is a very meaningful one. Part of the meaning will be readily appreciated by your people.

The principal guest at a meal or a meeting sits at the right hand of the host or the chair. That is the place of honour.

Jesus is in the place of supreme honour in relation to God in heaven. That is the first and obvious meaning still implied in our common usage to this day.

In the second place, if someone is described as 'so-and-so's right hand person' we know it means that that person is in closest proximity to the head – the head's first representative. Jesus, who was the nearest ever to God on earth, is the nearest to God in heaven. That meaning too will be readily understood.

There is a third meaning which might have been familiar to the first century Christians in the Roman Mediterranean world. In the Roman law courts the advocate for the defence sat on the right hand of the judge. Was this what was in the mind of the writer of I John when he wrote: 'If any one does sin, we have an advocate with the Father' (I John 2:1)?

The Ascension properly understood is an event of great comfort for sinful men and women hoping for heaven yet humbly doubting their qualification for entry.

O how shall I, whose native sphere
Is dark, whose mind is dim,
Before the Ineffable appear
And on my naked spirit bear
The uncreated beam?

There is a way for man to rise
To that sublime abode,
An offering and a sacrifice,
A Holy Spirit's energies,
An Advocate with God.

We have an advocate. He sits at the right hand of God.

In the words of the preamble in *The Worshipbook* lectionary to Eastertide (p 171): 'Ascension Day, forty days after Easter, is celebrated to affirm that Jesus Christ is Lord of all times and places.'

6

PENTECOST

WE turn now to preaching through Pentecost. This is the longest single section of the Christian Year and covers 27 Sundays. It begins with the day of Pentecost. The name is from the Jewish festival which takes its name from the fact that it falls fifty days after the Passover. The word means the fiftieth. The Sunday after Pentecost is normally called Trinity Sunday, and some denominations and some lectionaries renumber the Sundays after Trinity and call them the First Sunday After Trinity, the Second Sunday After Trinity, and so on. The tendency appears to be away from this practice, and for obvious reasons. It would be an awesome thought that for some 25 Sundays you should be required to preach on some aspect of the Trinity!

Some might find it equally restrictive to have to preach for twenty seven Sundays on the Holy Spirit. Some might even find it difficult enough to preach one sermon on the Holy Spirit on Whitsunday. That, by the way, is the alternative Christian name for the day of Pentecost, and the origin of the name is that that was a popular day in the early Church for catechumens to make their profession of faith and be confirmed. It was, and still is in some churches, a common custom for the confirmands to wear white, hence Whitsunday. I once spent a Whitsunday in Paris and I wandered into Notre Dame, where a confirmation service was in progress. The little girls wore white dresses, and the little boys a white carnation. I came across groups of boys and girls similarly adorned that morning as I walked through the city. Clearly it was confirmation day in many of the churches that

Whitsunday. This is in commemoration of the first Whitsunday when, according to the account of that Pentecost in Acts 2, some three thousand were added to the Church that day.

It should be noted that Acts 2:1-13 is the only lesson that the lectionary suggests should be read each year in the three-year course of lessons. On no other Sunday in the year is the repetition of the same lesson on the same Sunday for three consecutive years proposed. That is significant. It means that Acts 2:1-13 is *the locus classicus* for preaching on Whitsunday. You should not find this unduly restrictive or difficult. Of course, you are not required to take your text from the prescribed lesson, though there are good texts in this passage. There is no shortage of texts.

There is a sermon on obedience as a prerequisite of the coming of the Holy Spirit, the obedience of togetherness, in the opening words of the chapter: 'When the day of Pentecost had come, they were all together in one place,' as Jesus had instructed them.

There is the straightforward text which gives you plenty of room to work in: 'they were all filled with the Holy Spirit' (Acts 2:4).

A few years ago on a bus journey from Washington DC to Charlottesville I noticed a young fellow sitting near me reading a book with the striking title splashed across the cover: *These Are Not Drunken As Ye Suppose,* which is a text from this Whitsunday passage (Acts 2:15, KJV), and which provided me with the introduction to and the text for my Whitsunday sermon in my own church a few weeks later.

It may not be getting a text that worries you. Indeed, you can do without a text and simply expound the passage. But what are we to say about this event? Is this not very difficult? I believe that there have been times when it has been more difficult than at other times to preach on the Holy Spirit. But I do not think today is such a time. Fifty years ago the intellectual climate was rather arrogant. We believed in a world of strict cause and effect. It was a calculable world. It was a world in which the material was all that mattered. It was a world in which mystery was only something which we had not quite got round to discovering, but given time we would be able to produce a rational explanation for what was at present inexplicable. We had a hangover from the Swinburne materialistic romanticism expressed in the lines:

Glory to man in the highest,
For man is the master of things.

This is no longer descriptive of the intellectual climate of our time, despite our far greater mastery of things than Swinburne ever dreamed of. In part our overconfidence was shaken by the First World War, and perhaps even more by what happened after it, the breakdown of our economy and the consequences in stock market crashes, slumps, and unemployment. We began to think that perhaps we didn't know everything. We wondered where we were going.

Once I built a railroad,
Now it's done.
Buddy can you spare a dime?

But the chief reason for the change of climate was the integrity of scientists themselves, who began to find evidence that did not easily fit into a closed causal system. There had always been first-class scientists who allowed room for the contingent and the exceptional in their scientific thinking and who were hesitant about claiming too much for the scientific method. There was the work of Rhine at Duke University and the accounts of those experiments which led to the coining of the words 'extrasensory perception' (ESP) to describe the phenomenon. More recently and more popularly there appeared before the eyes of millions watching television the feats of Uri Geller, bending spoons, starting watches, and doing various experiments which seemed to point to forces which did not seem to work according to any known and accepted principle.

All that and more, both explicable and inexplicable, has produced a climate which is at least honestly agnostic and prepared to say to the sceptic, in the words of Hamlet:

> *There are more things in heaven and earth, Horatio,*
> *Than are dreamed of in your philosophy.*

And that climate at its best is open to consideration of the reality that we call the Holy Spirit.

That does not mean that it is easy to preach the Holy Spirit. Spirit by its very nature is difficult to grasp. There is nothing material to lay hold on. You cannot see Spirit. This must be frankly acknowledged. In an old Scots phrase, Spirit is 'better felt than tellt.' It is all the more important that the coming of the Holy Spirit should be earthed to the events of the first Whitsunday. It is also understandable why those who described the experience should use the terms they did. They said it was like the noise of a strong wind sweeping through the house. You may recall that Jesus used that analogy when speaking to Nicodemus (John 3:8). They said it was like forked lightning playing round each one of them. There was a fair commotion. Remember, this was another festival occasion, and there were Jews and proselytes from all over the Mediterranean world. There was bewilderment, amazement, astonishment, and perplexity – those words are all used in the text. And those that were filled with the Spirit spoke with tongues as the Spirit gave them utterance, and the people said: 'Are not all these who are speaking Galileans? And how is it that we hear, each of us in his own native language?' (Acts 2:7-8).

That is a question which is still being asked. I would ask you to note a few points. The first is that speaking with tongues in the sense of babbling is not an unknown phenomenon. Paul was cautious about it. He said that he would rather speak with understanding than babble. The second point is that it would appear that many of those there got the sense of what was said in the speaking with tongues. They don't give a translation, they give the sense of what they heard in general terms. It was 'the mighty works of God' (Acts 2:11). The third point is that others did not get any sense out of what they were saying and dismissed the initial speaking with tongues as the babbling of drunk men. The fourth point is that Peter's sermon which follows verse 13 was obviously given in straight speech. The speaking with tongues was and should be regarded as a peripheral phenomenon, not exclusive to that occasion but an unusual phenomenon which is occasionally experienced at times of great excitement and deep emotion. This was such an occasion. There were signs and phenomena which accompanied the coming of the Spirit on this occasion, and these and other signs have accompanied the coming of the Spirit on other occasions. 'The wind blows where it wills, and you hear the sound of it, but you do not know whence it comes or whither it goes; so it is with every one who is born of the Spirit' (John 3:8).

You have, I think, got to say something about those phenomena, in part because they did accompany the coming of the Spirit on the first Whitsunday, and in part because it is very understandable that people should be curious and should still ask: 'What does this mean?' I would make neither too much nor too little of what I have called the peripheral phenomena. It is important that nothing should detract from the reality of the coming of the Holy Spirit, and its more lasting effects. It is thoroughly biblical to urge that we test the Spirit, and you may remind your people that Paul warns us not to mistake the signs for the substance. He lists the fruits in writing to the Galatians: 'love, joy, peace, patience, kindness, goodness, faithfulness, gentleness, self-control' (Galatians 5:22-23). And in I Corinthians 12 you have some of the functions and gifts of the Spirit outlined. The passage is one which merits study and possibly a sermon on its own on one of the Sundays following Whitsunday.

In passing you may consider, sometime during a post-Pentecostal period, preaching through I Corinthians 13 in a series of sermons.

But, to return to Whitsunday, having dealt with the obedience to Christ's command, and the peripheral phenomena, you have to deal with the fulfilment of Christ's promise to send his Spirit.

It is important to recognise that the Holy Spirit is neither an invention of Jesus nor an extra which no one had ever experienced before. The air we breathe is always there, though we are more conscious of it when the air moves and stirs the leaves on the trees. The wind blows where it will, and you hear the sound and sough of it. So it is with the spirit. The Old Testament account of the beginning of things begins with the wind or Spirit of God moving over the vast void, bringing the cosmos out of chaos. The Spirit is the Creator Spirit filling all things.

That can be dangerously impersonal, and you may want to counteract that impression by directing attention to the Abraham saga or the Moses saga, where the God who speaks is both very spiritual and very personal. It is worth noting that the Old Testament passage from Joel quoted by Peter indicates that prophecy, the seeing of visions, and the dreaming of dreams are proper functions of the Spirit of God. 'This' – the coming of the Holy Spirit, he says – 'is what was spoken by the prophet' (Acts 2:16). On the first Sunday after Pentecost the Old Testament lesson is one of the great biblical passages describing the vision of Isaiah at the door of the Temple and the call addressed to him. This also is that same Spirit that came on the very first Whitsunday.

You will, if you preach on the subject of the Holy Trinity on the first Sunday after Pentecost, say something about the relationship between God the Father, God the Son, and God the Holy Spirit, but it would be well to emphasise before finishing your sermon on Whitsunday that the Holy Spirit was wholly incarnate in the man Christ Jesus, and that the test of the reality of the Spirit is its Christlikeness. According to Jesus' promise it is his Spirit that he sends to inspire our living, not just an ecstatic experience or a wild enthusiasm, but an awareness that with this experience hereafter 'it is no longer I who live, but Christ who lives in me' (Galatians 2:20).

Now about preaching on Trinity Sunday, the first Sunday after Pentecost.

As a very young minister I was invited in the absence of the minister to preach in the central church of Dundee, St Mary's. It was Trinity Sunday. I began the sermon with these words: 'This is Trinity Sunday, and my subject therefore is the doctrine of the Holy Trinity.' I had lunch at the manse after the service. The minister's wife told me that when I began my sermon with that sentence her heart went into her boots. I asked why, and she said it was because she had never heard anyone preach on the Holy Trinity. And I gathered that she thought that was a good thing. She then went on to say that she was surprised to find that it wasn't so bad as she had feared!

The reaction of the wife of the minister of Dundee on being invited to consider the doctrine of the Trinity is fairly representative of the attitude of most of us, including ministers. We seem to think of the Trinity as the thick darkness where God was, and are disinclined to attempt to penetrate the darkness.

But is it really as bad as that? And what are we to do about biblical passages which, whether they are early or late, refer to God the Father, the Son, and the Holy Spirit? And are we to stop singing hymns that are addressed to God in Three Persons, Holy Trinity? Or do we just decide to leave all that unexplored? I don't think we can, and I don't think it is so very difficult to preach an annual sermon which has implicitly or explicitly the Trinity as its theme. I am confident, as I remarked to that minister's wife, that, like Monsieur Jourdain in Molière's *Le Bourgeois Gentilhomme,* who discovered that for forty years he had been speaking prose without knowing it, she had more than once heard a sermon on the Trinity which may not have mentioned the word, but whose content was about God the Father, the Son, and the Holy Spirit.

Where do you begin with a sermon on the Trinity? It's a good idea to begin with the Bible and with the uncovering of the revelation of God there. The Bible begins with God, a caring Creator who is occasionally described as the Father before Jesus adopted that word as his favourite name for God.

In Jesus the Word became flesh. He reveals not a new God but a new dimension of God, a new depth of God. Above all he gives God a face, but we recognise there that this is the face of the God whom we have discerned dimly in the Old Testament. The coming, the attitudes, the teaching, the dying, and the rising of Jesus reveal God as we have not and cannot see him without Christ. He is not a second God. He is the same God.

But God knows and we know that that is not enough. Jesus lived and taught, died and rose 2000 years ago. The God we see in the Old Testament is a God who works. He is a God of action. He is not an idea. The Jesus we see in the Gospels is also a worker. 'My meat is to do the will of him that sent me, and to finish his work,' he said (John 4:34, KJV). See also his promise (John 16:12-15).

And the work goes on, and his continuing work we know as the Holy Spirit. Again not another God, but the same God who was at work in the beginning of the world and who entered the world at one point in time in the person of Jesus, and who now energises the world and men and women by his Holy Spirit.

That is how the doctrine of the Trinity began to be stated. And it was stated very early, before the canon of the New Testament was completed. The trouble began when attempts were made to define the relationship between God the Father, God the Son, and God the Holy Spirit. This was very much an effort by theologians influenced by Greek thought and using Greek concepts and categories. You may, and with profit, study their writings in the privacy of your study, but I do not advise you in this instance to take your studies and your conclusions on this matter into your pulpit. Rather should you frankly acknowledge to the congregation that God is still the great mystery.

But I think you must also suggest to them that all of us in becoming mature Christians recapitulate in our own experience the biblical revelation of God the Father, God the Son, and God the Holy Spirit, though not necessarily in that order.

Some, perhaps most, begin with the revelation of a God behind our world. And they may advance to the recognition of what he is like in Jesus Christ. And they may arrive at theological maturity through the experience of God as the Spirit at work in them and in the fellowship of others and in the world.

Again, it may not necessarily be in that order that the revelation of God in his fullness comes. To some he comes first through admiration of the man Jesus: compare the Roman centurion at the foot of the cross. To others, he comes through a growing sense of the numinous, of the plus quality to the created world. You get this in much of Wordsworth's poetry.

All I am saying is that the Trinity is not so remote from religious experience as we are inclined to imagine. And if you interpret and expand obvious texts such as those suggested in *The Worshipbook* from the Gospels and epistles for this Sunday, I would be surprised if your people did not recognise that they were Trinitarians in experience even if they had never realised that that was their theology, and with you and with all the ages they may 'Give unto the LORD the glory due unto his name' (Psalms 29:2; 96:8, KJV), even the name of the Father and of the Son and of the Holy Spirit.

When I told a friend what I was trying to do in this book and that I was at the point of dealing with preaching in the post-Pentecostal period, he remarked that he had found the most difficult Sundays were the 25 Sundays or so, almost exactly half the year, between Pentecost and Advent. He said that he longed for Advent, when he would again be back to dealing with the run-up to the mighty acts. I would not be surprised if others were to tell me that in this post Pentecostal period they had a freedom in their preaching which they welcomed, and which meant that they were not restricted in their theme. They could preach as the Spirit moved, or as their fancy dictated! Oddly, the same ones during this period might at some points feel that they were without much guidance from the Gospel events and be glad of the fact, yet at others they might feel adrift on a vast, uncharted sea, and that this was a burden.

There is the general guidance of the heading to Pentecost in *The Worshipbook* lectionary (p 172): 'The festival … [commemorates] the gift of the Holy Spirit to the church, and an extended season for reflecting on how God's people live under the guidance of his Spirit.' This would suggest that you continue in the book of Acts to look at the Church which grew and became established by the outpouring of the Spirit. It is perhaps a little surprising that that is not the direction in which the lectionary points in any of the series of three year lessons suggested. Here you might do worse than follow the hint in *The Worshipbook's* preface, which states with approval (p 6) that some 'will supply their own variations. To do so will be to please, not disappoint, those who have prepared the book'.

I have not previously mentioned a very good Reformed custom – preaching through a book of the Bible. This is a season which lends itself to this practice, and the book of Acts is a very appropriate choice. It is a book of sufficient variety to prevent a sameness in preaching. I would suggest that one year you might preach through chapters 2 to 12 and the following year preach through chapters 13 to 28.

You would, of course, plan your course of sermons before you begin. You might analyse the content of Peter's first Christian sermon and note the effect of it. Or you might find a sermon on the Three Notes of the True Church as stated in the Scots Confession and as found in Acts 2:42-45: (1) teaching, doctrine, preaching; (2) the sacraments; (3) the discipline of fellowship, having all things in common. All that is the church becoming alive. The book of Acts, especially in the early chapters, is full of incidents, dramatic confrontations and personal encounters.

- There is the cripple cured at the Beautiful Gate and what comes of that.
- There is the dilemma of the priests and Sadducees and their prohibition of preaching which brought forth the great and difficult word: 'We must obey God rather than men' (Acts 5:29).
- There is Ananias and his wife Sapphira.
- There is Gamaliel. Was his a sensible and honourable position, or was he playing safe? Gamaliel's is the case for moderation.
- There is the beginning of disunity: and note that it is ostensibly on grounds of race. And there is the beginning of persecution in the death of Stephen. That takes us to the beginning of chapter 8.
- And so, to Simon the Sorcerer who joined the Church and wanted the Spirit for the wrong reason.
- There is a striking contrast between Simon and the unnamed Ethiopian eunuch. Contrasts can be profitable material.
- Then there is the conversion of St Paul, and surely that other Ananias, who was obedient despite his fear and did his duty with grace, is a subject for a sermon. And as a postscript to that sermon you have the part played by Barnabas in introducing Paul to the disciples.
- And there is Cornelius, the Roman centurion, and the conviction to which Paul was led that the gospel was not for Jews only, which is the great breakthrough by the power of the Spirit, and which occupies most of chapters 10 and 11.

If you were to preach on all of the subjects I have touched on you would preach about a dozen sermons while reading through most of the first eleven chapters of Acts. I think if you are going to preach through any of the larger books of the Bible you should not have, at any one time, a consecutive series of more than about twelve sermons. The threshold of boredom of listeners listening to one book, even such a varied book as Acts, is not very high.

I leave you to work out your own series for the second half of Acts, which you might read through with your congregation another year at this time.

I see that for one year it is suggested that you read through Matthew's Gospel from chapter 9 onwards through the whole period. There is much to be said for this, but here again I would be inclined not to preach from one Gospel longer than for half the period in any one year. And again, the following year, I would take up where I had left off. You may think this would be more appropriate for a Sunday School class year and you may be right.

I especially emphasise this caution when you are preaching consecutively from the longer and more difficult letters of Paul. Romans, for example, for 16 consecutive Sundays might be too much. True!!

Sometimes you should not be ashamed to paint with a large brush. You might well read through Romans with the congregation on 16 Sundays, but give them in three or four sermons the gist of what Paul is saying in writing to the Romans. It is worth considering doing this not only with some of the letters, but also with some of the prophets. You could, of course, divide Isaiah and preach on the different Isaiahs on three successive years. (The length of the series would probably vary considerably.)

This is a period when you might uncover for people some of the truths and riches contained in the Old Testament. There was a time, not so long ago, when preaching from the Old Testament was neglected. It should not be neglected. It was our Lord's Bible, and he quotes extensively from it, especially from the prophets and from the Psalms.

And if you ask me: 'Where should I begin?', I can see nothing wrong with the simple answer: 'At the beginning.' You will have to wrestle with some of the profound questions raised in the first four chapters of Genesis:

- How the world began.
- Our place in relation to the animal kingdom and the

marvellous picture of God bringing the animals for Adam to name.

- Man and woman – Adam and Eve.
- Original sin – the serpent in Eden.
- The human family divided – Cain and Abel.

Then there are the sagas:

- The Noah saga.
- The Abraham and Isaac saga (perhaps over two years).
- The Jacob and Esau saga.
- The Joseph saga ... and many more.

I should not need to add two notes of caution, but I will. One: you don't need to tell your congregation everything that is recorded about Old Testament characters. They can read. You have to select what helps to edify. I am not suggesting that you gloss over the drunkenness of Noah or David's affair with Bathsheba and what came of it. Rather, I am suggesting that you do not, for example, try to preach on the text which tells us David was ruddy and of a fair countenance. Eschew the *outré*. And the second note: don't take more than one Old Testament series in any one year; or if you do, don't take two sagas in one year. Take a saga and a synopsis of one of the prophets, concentrating not so much on the character but on the message and its relevance for us today. Or a saga and the message of, say, selected Psalms, might appropriately go together in a year's preaching.

I commend the Psalms to you because preaching is about the human experience of the divine. It is in and to human experience that God reveals himself. And the Psalms are in all their variety the expression of how men found God. You should, of course, have an introduction to the first sermon giving an account of the Psalms, 'the praises', as they are called in the Hebrew. You could make a not-very-precise analogy between our hymnbook and the psalter. Certainly just as our hymnbook is a collection with different theological insights spanning the centuries and drawing contributions from all the ages, so the psalter similarly is a collection from the earliest Jewish period until some four hundred years before the Christian period. You should know what the scholars have found out about the Psalms, or for that matter any book of the Bible that you are going to preach from. But you should not dazzle your congregation with the extent of your knowledge. They won't be dazzled. They will be dazed. Or they will doze. Or they will think of something else and leave you to walk the path of learning alone. Give them enough to have an understanding of the background, and if at all possible tell them what has relevance to their own situation. They have a hymn-book. So had the Jews. Something they can immediately latch on to. You might even add that many Christians have, with profit to their devotional life, used their hymnbook to speak to God and to speak to others as from God in much the same way as Jews and Christians throughout the ages have used the Psalms.

Sometimes a line or a particular verse of a hymn has a special appeal for you. Sometimes a hymn is an entity which speaks to you as a whole.

You will find that it is the same with the Psalms. You will, I hope, preach on great familiar Psalms which are whole entities, like Psalm 23 or 121 – both personal Psalms; as well as Psalm 67 or 90 – both great general utterances. This is one of the marvellous things about the Psalms. They have an astonishing range because the human heart has an astonishing range and God is infinite. There are verses in the Psalms that are a profound yet touchingly simple witness to faith and to God's response.

We all know 'The LORD is my shepherd', but how many know the Psalm which precedes it, with its splendid assurance, 'Upon thee was I cast from my birth, and since my mother bore me thou hast been my God' (Psalm 22:10)? That is the faith behind pedobaptism, and – though I will be speaking about preaching on sacramental occasions later – I offer you that as a text for such an occasion. But not only for that occasion, but for the occasion that comes to us all when we feel that we are of no account.

There are many comfortable words in the Psalms. There are simple testimonies: 'I was brought low, and he helped me' (Psalm 116:6, KJV). 'Wait on the LORD: be of good courage, and he shall strengthen thine heart: wait, I say, on the LORD' (Psalm 27:14, KJV). 'This poor man cried, and the LORD heard him' (Psalm 34:6, KJV) – is almost surprised. Shouldn't we always be surprised by God? There is the magnificent conjoint statement in Psalm 147:3-4 (KJV): 'He healeth the broken in heart, and bindeth up their wounds.' 'He telleth the number of the stars; he calleth them all by their names.' The Creator is the Comforter. The Comforter is the Lord God Almighty. The greatness of God is that he is both.

And there are Psalms of penitence: Psalm 139 and Psalm 51 – which may or may not be by David after Bathsheba – are two of the greatest. They speak for and to every sorry sinful soul.

And the occasional outburst – the bitterness of the exile in Psalm 137, and the protests of Psalms 77 and 82, when with boldness the Psalmist questions God. The congregation will question God. You will question God at times. The psalmist in questioning often echoes our questioning, and sometimes also provides an answer, even if it is only to go on questioning. It is a blessed thing to inquire in his temple.

You will, I am sure, come back again and again to the Psalms.

The New Testament also has its poetry, and you should not neglect that. When Paul has done with the various callings to which the Spirit calls us he concludes – and note that is the context – with the great hymn to love in I Corinthians 13. You may preach one or two sermons on this chapter, possibly a series of three, but I don't think you should do more than that at any one time. You don't dissect poetry. If you do you kill it. But since this, according to Paul, is the most excellent fruit of the Spirit, it is especially appropriate at this season.

And so are sermons on the theme of the Church. It is significant that the Apostles' Creed – and others – follow confession of faith in the Holy Spirit with faith in the Church:

I believe in the Holy Ghost;
The holy Catholic Church.

The Church is a consequence of the Spirit.

There is also the fact that this is the time of the year when people return to their communities from holiday. Schools and colleges begin their term after the summer break. The life of the Church, which should be the heart and inspiration of the community for those who belong to it, begins to quicken. Its organisations resume their meetings. The programs which have been planned are put into operation.

You may think, and you may be right, that much of what I have just said might be more fitting for such programs. This is a time for thinking about what it is all for. It is a time for commitment and rededication.

It is also a time for criticism of the Church which is reformed yet *semper reformanda.*

Perhaps the best place to begin is with one of the suggested Gospel lections for the fourteenth Sunday after Pentecost. In that Caesarea Philippi conversation in Matthew 16, there is Jesus' question, the question he puts to everyone. It is again the Advent question: 'Who is this?'

The answers are varied: 'John the Baptist ... Elijah ... Jeremiah or one of the prophets.' It is comparatively easy to get that kind of human estimate of Jesus. 'The best man who ever lived' ... 'a great teacher' ... 'a superb moralist' ... 'an ethical philosopher of the highest rank.'

But Jesus was not and is not content with that kind of compliment. It is only when we confess that Jesus is the Messiah, the Son of the living God, God down to earth, that he knows that his Church is well founded on a rock. And this conviction is not something one arrives at by human learning. It is something that comes home to you. This is what God is like. God is like Jesus. Jesus is like God.

You may go on to point out that that confession of faith

by Peter was followed by Peter's trying to tell Jesus what was to be. He was not to be crucified and to rise again. That was not how it was to be. That was not how he was to save the world and justify God. And Peter, who was called a foundation stone of the Church, was also called a devilish stumbling block.

Or you may prefer to do as the lectionary suggests, and devote another sermon to this truth that the Church is at one and the same time formed from ordinary men and women who are seized of the revelation of God and who yet never quite lose their varied expressions of human weakness and sin and are a stumbling block to Christ and his kingdom. Through lack of understanding of this, many become despairing of themselves and disillusioned with the Church. You have to deal with this, pointing not only to the frailties of the first disciples – most of whom according to this passage had not gotten beyond thinking of Jesus as just another holy man – but also to the cooling enthusiasm of Ananias and his wife, the fearfulness of Timothy, and the disastrous state of the early church at Corinth as shown in Paul's two letters to the Corinthians.

Yet the Church is the Body of Christ, and it is by grace that we are saved through faith and that not of ourselves. It is a matter for perpetual astonishment that Jesus Christ should choose and can transform the very frail, raw material that humanity is – *massa perditionis* – and can and does use us to build his Church, against which the gates of hell shall not prevail.

There is a great tendency to criticise the Church among ministers and members alike, and that is no bad thing provided we remember and we remind our people individually and collectively that there is no instance in the New Testament of anyone becoming a Christian, a follower of Jesus Christ, and remaining outside the fellowship of the Church.

With all its faults it is the Church that has preserved and passed on the gospel. True, it has at times presented an unbalanced gospel, sometimes a distorted gospel, sometimes even a perverted gospel. And its presentation of the gospel, unbalanced in one place and at one time, has often been equally lopsided in the opposite direction in another place or at another time. Even so, it has preserved the gospel and kept the light of truth alive always by the mysterious working of the Holy Spirit.

Criticism is no bad thing, also provided it is constructive and born of love of the Church. Christ loved the Church and gave himself for it. If we love him, we love his Church too and give ourselves wholeheartedly for its service.

You will at times ask yourself in Pauline terms: 'Despise ye the church of God?' (I Corinthians 11:22, KJV) and it is a good question to put to your people. One of the few sermons I remember reading many years ago was by Henry Emerson Fosdick, and it was on that text. It was a fine apologia – which is not the same thing as an apology – for the Church. I recall that Fosdick suggested that it would be patently foolish for people to say they believed in education but had no use for educational institutions, schools and colleges. Or for people to say that they were all for law and order, but would scrap the officers of the law and the law courts. Is it not equally absurd to suggest that we believe in religion, we believe in Jesus Christ, but we can do without the institution of the Church, his institution, his Church? Certainly all our institutions, educational, legal, medical, and financial, require the most stringent scrutiny and the most searching criticism, but no community can live for long without them. And the same is true of the Church. The Christian community must constantly have the Church under criticism and reappraisal at all levels, and not least at the congregational level, but that Christian community cannot last long without the Church of the living God, the pillar and ground of the truth.

One final suggestion for this end period of the Pentecostal season that I would make when dealing with the Church is that you might consider a series of seven sermons on the letters to the seven churches in the book of Revelation. Since the letters are short, and, as you cannot fail to notice, since there is some repetition in what is said to the churches in the various places, you may find it convenient on one or more Sundays to take the message to two of the churches as your theme. The series could be reduced in that way to six or five or four sermons.

I have never preached such a series, but on rereading the letters to the seven churches I detect a sermonic pattern. Each letter has something to say in favour of the recipient church. Each also has something to say about its weakness. And each letter concludes with an exhortation. In four of the letters that is the order of the construction of the letter. In the other three the emphasis on the weakness of the church comes first.

This can be set out [plus (+), minus (−), and therefore (∴)] as follows:

	+	−	∴
Ephesus	Toil and fortitude.	Love grown cold.	Repent.
Smyrna	− Hard-pressed and poor.	+ Spiritually rich.	Fear not.
Pergamum	+ Confronting a wicked world.	− Temptation to permissiveness.	Receive the hidden manna.
Thyatira	+ Love, faith, service.	− Self-satisfied.	Persevere.
Sardis	− Reputed living, but dead.	+ Good there: to be encouraged.	Work on it.
Philadelphia	+ Open door of opportunity.	− Small strength.	Hold on.
Laodicea	− Neither hot nor cold lukewarm, 'make God sick.'	+ Spirit still pleads; God rebukes those he loves.	Open the door and let God in.

When preaching on the Church and to the Church, avoid the scolding and the whining note. The pronoun to use is 'we' not 'you'. Together *we* are the Church, all of us, every one a member, and every one part of the glory and the shame of the Church.

Finally, let me emphasise, you may be reading through a Gospel or a book of the Bible and find that a chapter or two have nothing to say to you. Then my advice is – skip it! If, however, one sentence or passage speaks to you, that and that in itself is enough to be going on with – then, get on with it.

7

Sacraments and Ordinances

YOU will frequently be preaching on occasions when the sacraments are celebrated. Less frequently, but inevitably, you will have to preach at a confirmation, or at an ordination. You may be asked to preach at a marriage, or at a funeral, or an In Memoriam service.

Many ministers find that preaching on such occasions is very difficult, the difficulty being only exceeded by deciding what to preach on what are described in *The Worshipbook* as 'Special Days', ranging from New Year's Day to Thanksgiving Day, and which I propose to deal with in the next chapter.

There are two theories about how to tackle the problem of special occasions, whether sacred or secular. One is virtually to ignore them in the sermon and to make appropriate reference to the special occasion in the prayers. This is to accept the advice given to a young minister by an older minister. In answer to the query, 'What should I preach about on such occasions?', the reply of the older man was: 'God and twenty minutes.' It is a valid if not very helpful reply, and the time allotted is excessive for weddings and funerals, where five to ten minutes should suffice. There are occasions when it is appropriate and sufficient to make a reference to the special occasion at the *beginning* of the sermon, or – since the Action usually follows – at the *end* of the sermon for such occasions as the sacraments, confirmation, and ordination.

The other theory about preaching on such occasions is that the sermon should be wholly directed to the occasion. In my view you need not adhere slavishly to one theory or the other. Clearly if you are celebrating holy communion or holy baptism once a month or more frequently, you would soon exhaust both the theology of the sacraments and your congregation if on every occasion you were to devote the entire sermon to an exposition of the meaning of the sacrament.

But, that having been said, my impression is that few preachers are in any danger of overdoing direct preaching on sacramental occasions, and it is perfectly possible to listen to a year's preaching on sacramental occasions which contains a minimal content of sacramental doctrine and sometimes no content at all. This is contrary to the New Testament practice and to the Reformed tradition.

In the New Testament, in the book of Acts for example, you will find that the Church met to listen to the apostles' doctrine and for the breaking of bread. The two went together. Similarly with baptism: this took place after exposition and declaration of the gospel. One of the complaints of the Reformers against the decayed Roman Catholic Church was that there was no preaching at the mass. It was a spectacle, and because of the lack of preliminary preaching it had become a superstitious rite. It was this rather than proper doctrinal preaching which led to the cruder forms of transubstantiation teaching. Even Luther found it difficult to get away from this in its literal form. His consubstantiation theory is no solution. Calvin, that very rational man, was nearer the truly Catholic doctrine when he stood as firmly as anyone for the Real Presence in the sacrament, and when he acknowledged: 'It is too high a mystery either for my mind to comprehend or my words to express ... I feel it, rather than understand it.' John Knox's position is set out by Eustace Percy in a correct observation which is worth quoting: Knox's 'conception of the central act of Christian worship (*ie* the Lord's Supper) set a lasting seal upon the Church of Scotland, differentiating it from all other Protestant communions and making it, in the strict sense of the term, a Eucharistic Church'

(Lord Eustace Percy: *John Knox* [Richmond: John Knox], no date, p 56). In the Scots Confession, which Knox had a hand in drafting, there is a strong condemnation of 'the vanity of those who affirm the sacraments to be nothing else but naked and bare signs,' and the clear affirmation, 'we must assuredly believe that the bread which we break is the communion of Christ's body and the cup which we bless is the communion of his blood'. The Scots Confession then goes on to caution us that those blessings received in the sacraments are not given to us apart from the word. And it is clear that what they normally meant by that was that the word preached should accompany the sacrament. We are ministers of the word and sacraments, and we should hold the unity of our office by the practice of our preaching, even if at the end of all our words we have to say with Paul, 'O the depth', and acknowledge with Calvin that it is a 'high mystery'.

In passing let me say that I have noted that *The Worshipbook* agrees with the New Testament in suggesting that it is fitting that the Lord's Supper be celebrated each Lord's Day. Calvin wanted that at Geneva, but had to settle for a monthly celebration, and I imagine that that is becoming the practice in America. It is increasingly so in Scotland; only a few of our congregations have adopted the New Testament practice. But more are doing so.

But whatever the practice is, and however frequently or infrequently holy communion is celebrated, we have a duty to instruct our people as best we can about the meaning of holy communion. This is not easy, but my experience is that such teaching is both required and appreciated, and, as I have suggested, it is underdone rather than overdone.

In my first parish I preached through the words of the institution of the sacrament as recorded by Paul in I Corinthians 11:23-26. I did this in four sermons over the four quarterly communions, which was the normal number of celebrations sixty years ago. I continued this practice in my subsequent pastorates – though not the same sermons! My division of the passage was as follows:

1 *'The Lord Jesus on the night when he was betrayed.'*
   This text I have touched on in the Holy Week chapter. It is
   also most significant for the meaning of holy communion.
   This is not something we do. It is something that Christ
   does. It also establishes the historical foundation of the
   sacrament. It takes us back to the Upper Room.

2 *'Took bread, and when he had given thanks, he broke it, and said,
   "This is my body which is for you, do this in remembrance of me".'*
   There is much here for you to ponder and develop, and I leave
   you to do so. This it is that gives body to the sacrament.

3 *'In the same way also the cup, after supper, saying, "This cup is the
   new covenant in my blood".'*
   Here you would preach on the significance of the cup and
   the new covenant. This gives spirit.

4 And finally: *'For as often as you eat this bread and drink the cup,
   you proclaim the Lord's death until he comes.'*
   This relates the communion to the perpetual benefits of
   the death of Jesus and to his second coming and the con-
   summation of all things in him.

In the preface by Principal Wishart, Principal of Edinburgh
University, to a book of Action sermons – that is, sermons
accompanying a sacrament, an ordination, or a confirmation –
published in 1774, there is this sentence: 'In this ordinance we
are to call to mind the most glorious things God either hath
done or will do for his people: so in the right use of it we par-
take of the greatest benefits we can enjoy here on earth, and are
confirmed in the faith and hope of those we look for hereafter
in heaven.'

I see no reason why if there is a monthly celebration such an
exposition as I have outlined should not be done at four successive monthly communions.

If holy communion is celebrated on any of the great festivals, the main theme of the sermon would be the theme appropriate to the festival, but it is not difficult to relate the sacrament to the festivals, and it is important that the congregation should realise the relevance of the sacrament to the festival.

It is also important to expound the structure of the service of holy communion so that people can follow the various parts of the service. This could be done, I suppose, in one sermon, but it would be better done as part of a series on the structure of, say, the morning service and leading up to a sermon on the structure of the communion service. That could cover a month's preaching. It seems to me that we do not do enough to help our people participate with understanding in the services of the Church. Participation in the services by the people was part of the aim of the Reformers. This means more than singing hymns and saying responses. It means, among other things, an under-standing of the doctrine of the forgiveness of sin, which is why we have a prayer of confession and why we should have a declaration of pardon. There is a great need for teaching on prayer, not least on prayers of intercession, and a series of sermons on the structure of the service would provide an opportunity for sharing with your people an understanding of the privilege and problems of prayer. It would also give an occasion for discussing the place of music in the services of the Church – something we don't think enough about. And in such a service there would have to be a sermon on sermons. Again this is something we don't think enough about with our people.

To return to preaching Action sermons: you should, of course, find texts and contexts in the accounts of the Lord's Supper in the Gospels. And in St John's Gospel the dispute among the disciples about who was the greatest, the washing of the disciples' feet, and the eucharistic prayer, are especially appropriate as themes for sermons at holy communion.

And there are, of course, frequent references both in the book of Acts and in other letters than I Corinthians to the fact and the significance of the sacrament. Those references can be a fruitful source and a useful starting point for sermons suitable to the occasion. Nor should you feel confined to the New Testament in looking for a text or a theme to point to the sacrament. Psalm 34:8 invites us to 'taste and see that the LORD is good', and in Psalm 23:3 the psalmist assures us that 'he restores my soul', and that surely is what the bread and the wine of the sacrament are for. It is in the Old Testament that we find the origin of the Passover, which, as Paul points out, is related to the crucial act of Christ which we remember in the sacrament of holy communion.

I hope you will often preach on baptism when you celebrate the sacrament of baptism. This is purely a gospel sacrament, especially when, as is common in our church, the baptism is the baptism of an infant. Here is an amazing statement of the mystery of prevenient grace, not, as you will point out, necessarily tied to the moment or act of administration, but revealing of the intention and goodwill of God in his love for us. This you must proclaim, and this you must expound, while recognising humbly that you cannot explain it. Here too you must reaffirm that the act of baptism is not a bare sign but is a recognition of something done by Christ which passes knowledge and which is expressed in a sign because it cannot be fully expressed in words alone. But here again word and sacrament ought to go together, the one illuminating the other, the word expounding the meaning of the sacrament and the sacrament illustrating the word. And, remember, the word in New Testament terms is always a deed, never just an idea. It is this fact that gives congruity to word and sacrament. Baptism is an expression of amazing grace.

Again it is clear from the book of Acts and from the letters that this was the practice of the early Church. There was, either individually, as in the case of the Ethiopian, or collectively, as in the cases of the Philippian jailer and Lydia, an exposition of the Christian faith prior to baptism, and it is in that faith and into that faith that baptism in the name of the Father and of the

Son and of the Holy Ghost takes place. Any or all of the instances recorded in the New Testament can provide suitable texts and contexts for sermons on baptism. Nor should you neglect to make the case for pedobaptism, which is theologically sound even though there is no indisputable case of infant baptism in the New Testament. In this connection it has always seemed to me that the passage in the Gospels in which we are told that Jesus took children into his arms and blessed them is relevant. Was that a sentimental action? Or were the children blessed? And can the blessing of God in Christ in baptism be helped to be effectual or subsequently inhibited? We do not believe *ex opero operato*.

The sacraments are always both personal and social, and this is obviously so in baptism when celebrated in the face of the congregation:

- There are the parents, the family.
- There is the congregation, the family of God.
- There is the child.
- There is the living, loving God whose Son said, 'Go therefore ... baptising ... [and] teaching'.

These are the *dramatis personae* of baptism.

On baptismal occasions you may preach on the importance of the family and in particular the duties of parents. You should also, on occasions, emphasise the duties and responsibilities of the congregation to provide Christian education and to create a Christian community. You should underline the significance of baptism, and especially infant baptism, for the Christian doctrine of human nature. But above all, and again and again, you should see in this sacrament, and help your people to see, something of the length, breadth, depth, and height of the love of God which is in Christ Jesus our Lord.

Here again I would urge you not to neglect the Old Testament as a source of baptismal texts and themes. The practice of circumcision, as Paul realised, has some relevance to infant baptism. And, in this connection, do not fail to point out how specifically Christian is the fact that we baptise girls as well as boys. And there are many family stories in the Old Testament which can be held up as either an example or a warning when stressing the importance of the family in baptism. There is the story of the infant Moses. There is the story of Jacob and Esau. There is the unwise favouritism shown by the mother of Benjamin and by the father of Joseph. There is the infant Samuel, and Hannah's dedication of her son to the Lord. And much more – including some sayings in the book of Proverbs about children – which you will no doubt discover for yourself.

Marriage in our tradition is not called a sacrament but a divine ordinance, and you may occasionally be invited, or it may be your wish, to preach a sermon during the marriage service. If you do, I commend to your attention the rubric in *The Worshipbook* (p 66) which reads: 'The minister may deliver a brief Sermon on the lessons from Scripture.' I would like to underline the verb 'may deliver'. Don't be too ready to feel a compulsion to preach a sermon. It is an option perhaps better exercised by omission rather than commission. If you occasionally do preach a sermon be sure that the adjective 'brief' can be applied to your effort. On no account should you begin the congratulatory speeches in the middle of the marriage service as a substitute for a sermon. Congratulatory speeches are properly kept for the reception. As the rubric wisely suggests, and I would underline, the sermon should be, if there is a sermon, 'on the lessons from Scripture'.

My own preference would be for a preamble similar to the preamble to the marriage in the former *Book of Common Order*, which sets out briefly and yet adequately the Christian view of marriage.

In addition to the lessons from Colossians 3 and I Corinthians 13 – which personally I would be inclined to transpose as lessons to be read before rather than after the vows – you may find appropriate lessons in whole or in part in Psalms 127 and 128;

Proverbs 31:10-31; Ephesians 5:21-23; I John 4:7-18; and from the Gospel of John 15:9-13, which I think should come after the vows.

I believe you will find material for an appropriate brief sermon in any of those passages, but there are other texts which are suitable and which you may discover for yourselves which you may expand and apply to marriage.

One of the most important services at which you will have to preach is the service which in *The Worshipbook* (p 48) is headed 'The Commissioning of Baptised Members; the Order for Their Confirmation; and the Reception of Members from Other Churches'. Do I detect a degree of uneasiness about the use of terms here? 'Commissioning of Baptised Members' is doubtless the same as 'the Order for their Confirmation'. In some churches the phrase used is 'Admission to First Communion'. I think this is playing with words. I don't mind what phrase is used so long as you avoid the words 'Joining the Church'. Those who are baptised are already members of the Church by virtue of their baptism into the name of the Father, the Son, and the Holy Spirit. I have never been able to understand the objection to the word 'confirmation'. It has the merit of antiquity, and Presbyterian antiquity as well as Catholic antiquity. But more than that, it seems to me to describe very well what this service is about. It is about persons confirming and affirming the faith into which they have been baptised. The terms of the preamble in the former *Book of Common Order* made this clear: 'God in his mercy has brought you to years of responsibility, and you have now come to acknowledge before God and His Church the covenant then made on your behalf, to profess your faith in the Lord Jesus, to consecrate yourself to Him, and thereby to bind yourselves anew to His service.' The wording may require modernisation, but it is an adequate description of the action that is to follow. You may do that – the rubrics are not Holy writ.

Where the persons about to profess their faith have not been baptised I have in recent years persuaded all such not to be separated from those with whom they have been meeting as catechumens, but to take their vows along with the others and then to be baptised and confirmed simultaneously in the face of the congregation. If and when this is done, adjustment in the preamble is necessary but can be done quite simply. I would commend this practice to you, and I can say that both those baptised as adults and the congregation have found this not just an acceptable practice, but a moving experience.

I am very glad to see that in *The Worshipbook* part of this service may include a welcome to members from other churches. It is most appropriate that this should be done at this service and, indeed, that the whole service should be one at which all members should, even if silently, renew their vows and their commitment to Christ and his Church.

It is such a commitment to Christ and his Church that is the general theme of the sermon on this occasion. Here you speak concerning Christ and the Church. The range of such a theme is very wide indeed. But you do not simply speak of Christ and the Church in general terms. Here men and women are committing themselves to Christ and his Church – and nowadays in my experience the age limits are very wide.

In recent years I have confirmed a man of seventy and a couple in their early fifties. In this connection I might mention that, when I thought it right, I have intimated that the class in preparation for confirmation is for adults. It came to me in Africa that many of those starting their life work for one reason or another – university, nursing training, *etc* – had missed the normal age and might be embarrassed in a group of possibly much younger people. I was astonished at the response. After I left Africa I was colleague to a friend in a great Edinburgh church. I told him about my experiment. He said, 'Right. You take the seniors and I will take the juniors and then we'll confirm them together.' We did with more seniors than juniors! A dominant note will be commitment, personal commitment. You may go to the Gospels for your examples of commitment to

Christ. There is the response of the disciples to the invitation, 'Follow me'. You may take the call of the Twelve collectively and indicate how individual they were and how different. Or you may take one – Matthew, for example – called where he was, as he was, and who made a ready response. Some of them were very ordinary, so ordinary that almost half of them have nothing remarkable about them. But they committed themselves. And there are many other examples outside the Twelve whom Jesus called, and some responded and some did not. You may inquire why they did not.

You may find the conversion of Paul providing you with material for a sermon in which you might point out that this experience was real and dramatic and led to a sudden change, or an apparently sudden change, and that while this kind of experience still happens, Paul's conversion is not typical of conversion in the New Testament.

What commitment to Christ and his Church means finds innumerable illustrations in passages from Paul's letters. I indicate only a few such passages which seem to me especially appropriate to confirmation: Romans 6; and 15:1-13; I Corinthians 1; three or four passages from 2 Corinthians 3 to 5, which includes the great claim of 5:17; Galatians 1; and 5:13-26; Ephesians 1:1-14; 2:1-10; 3; 4:17-32; and 6:10-24; Philippians 2:3-13; Colossians 1.

Those or other passages and texts are ones you can expound, and so keep before, not just those to be confirmed, but all your congregation this high calling through Christ Jesus.

Ordination, whether to the eldership or to the ministry, presents to the preacher another opportunity to preach 'concerning Christ and the Church', and several of the passages suggested as starting points for the sermon at confirmation may be found equally suitable for a sermon on the occasion of ordination.

But there are many passages that have particular relevance to the eldership, as, for example, I Thessalonians 5:12-28; I Timothy 3:1-13; 5:13 to 6:12; and I Peter 5. Others have general or particular relevance to the ministry, as, for example, 2 Timothy 1:1-4; and 2.

You should at some suitable occasion preach on the structure of the Presbyterian Church, disentangling as best you can the development of episcopal, conciliar, and congregational forms of government and what can be said in favour of each, pointing out that it would appear that our Lord did not lay down one dominical form of government for his Church, and that at their best the Reformers only claimed that our form of government was agreeable to the Word of God. Perhaps surprisingly, people are interested in structures, and it is our business to engage their interest. Jesus' parable about new wine requiring new structures is a possible starting point for such a sermon. Developments this century towards a structure of Church government combining elements from the main three types, may be an indication of the shape of things to come. And this development is increasingly being evidenced not only in, for example, the Church of South India, but at the grassroots level by churches in one locality yet of different denominations working together towards unity. Is this not the work of the Spirit of him who prayed repeatedly that his followers might be one?

Dedication of Church workers to various functions will demand special sermons, and here again some of the texts and topics already mentioned may prove equally suitable for this purpose. The command of our Lord to 'go therefore ... teaching' may be an obvious text for a sermon to Church school teachers, but need not be passed over simply because it is so obvious. One of the names people called Jesus was 'Teacher'. James 3 is also very relevant to teachers. You may occasionally have to preach to a school or student congregation. There is always a danger of thinking that you have to get on to their 'wavelength'; and an even greater danger, especially in preaching to schools, is to attempt to get down to their level. Certainly your duty is to engage their interest, and you may be able to do so by taking some dramatic incident, recapitulating it, asking questions about it, and drawing the lessons from it. I think, for example, of the account of Abraham about to sacrifice Isaac, or David at the cave of Adullam, or Elijah and the priests of Baal. There is much to appeal to the lively social conscience of the young in the book of Amos, and for comparison you could take the text from Isaiah of Jesus' first sermon at Nazareth. I have on a university occasion preached on the transfiguration as the confrontation of law and prophecy, and Jesus Christ the reconciler of the two opposing stances. There is always a tension, felt by the young, between those who are all for law and order and those who are all for protest. A problem, of which they are aware, is how to hold the two together – one of the major problems of our society. Nor should you avoid a saying of Jesus like: 'Except a man be born again, he cannot see the kingdom of God.' And, if you do choose such, please preach on the whole text and in its context. The appeal to be born again *in order that you may see the kingdom of God* and work for it, has a much greater appeal to young people than the appeal to be born again as if that were an end in itself. There are also many passages both in the Old Testament and in the New which present a *weltanschauung,* a world view, which, in faith, try to make sense of the world, and this is a theme which has an appeal to youth. Genesis 1:1 in the Old Testament and Romans 8:22, I would offer as examples. But you can waste much time and thought on special occasions in looking desperately for relevance and what will appeal, when perhaps what is required is simply to continue with your job of preaching the Gospel and teaching the way of Christ, and in the prayers commending them and their special concerns and circumstances to God.

What I have just said is also applicable to the sermon on In Memoriam occasions. More often than not, you will find that you are already advanced in your sermon preparations for a Sunday when you may have to announce to the congregation the death of one of their number. Normally this announcement and any tribute to be paid is best done before the intercessions, and you would then naturally lead people in appropriate prayers. You will also discover that there are few sermons to which a paragraph cannot be added which would lead up to the announcement and the tribute, or in which the tribute itself may refer back to what has been said in the sermon. When the funeral service takes place before the Sunday, a tribute may be made at the funeral, when appropriate, but it is very rarely appropriate to preach a sermon, and, if you feel you must, brevity is desirable. Similarly at special In Memoriam services on a weekday it is customary for someone, not necessarily the minister, to give a panegyric, but not to have a sermon.

When an In Memoriam service on a Sunday is appropriate, then the sermon should be suitable to the occasion. The practice of having In Memoriam services varies from congregation to congregation. In a small congregation where everybody knows everybody else and there is a strong family feeling, it may be possible to make sympathetic reference to every death which occurs within the family of God represented by that congregation. But where the congregation is large this is not so easy, and there has to be a limiting policy. It may be wise to confine Sunday In Memoriam services to officers of the congregation. You will find it useful to have a rule – though a good minister will judge when it would be right and agreeable to the congregation to make exception to the rule because of special circumstances, or because of a sense of loss felt by the congregation or community or nation as a whole.

The content of a sermon, you will find increasingly, is determined in no small measure by the congregation to which you are preaching, and this is particularly true of In Memoriam sermons. Much of what you say and how you say it will depend on the circumstances and on your sensitivity to the feelings of your congregation. You will also have special regard to the feelings of the mourners most nearly affected by the death of the person being commemorated. You must not harrow them.

On some occasions you will find that the character of the

person suggests to you a biblical text or character as a suitable subject for his or her In Memoriam. There are women in every congregation of whom the biblical phrase 'a mother in Israel' is an appropriate description. On the death of such a one, an examination of that phrase, its meaning, and the value of what that means to the natural family, to the family of God, and to the community might be appropriate. There are men in every congregation of whom at their passing it could be said, as was said of Enoch: 'Enoch walked with God.' You could develop that and apply it in various ways. To walk with someone means that you are going in the same direction, at the same pace, and you arrive at the same destination.

You will on occasion have to speak to a congregation burdened by sorrow because of some sad tragedy. My experience is that God's promise is true, and that on such occasions the word to speak will be given to you. There are times when the simple straightforward word is the best word – an exhortation, for example, to 'cast their burden on the Lord' in the sure faith that he will sustain them. A word like that recognises the burden of life, that it is burdensome. Our Lord warned us that in the world we will have tribulation, but he also assured us that we will be sustained and that he has overcome the world. Never pretend either that there is no such thing as tragedy or that we can always understand the reason why, and yet never leave your people without the assurance – the guarantee of which is the cross and resurrection of Christ – that God triumphs over tragedy, and that through faith in him we too are given the victory over defeat and death.

Of course, do not neglect to expound and preach on great biblical passages: on the death of Moses – the unfulfilled life; or on the death of Joshua – the final challenge of a warfare ending. The Psalms are a rich quarry because so many of them are concerned with questions of life and death. In addition to great and familiar Psalms like Psalms 23, 90 and 139, there are occasions when you may find that Psalms 22, 27, 40, 77, 102, 103, 115 and several sections of Psalm 119 are helpful, and those are only a few to begin with. There are many others which may provide you with the starting point of a text, as Psalms 13:3-6, 116:8 and 130:5. And again those are only a few that come to mind.

There are also chapters 14 and 17 in the book of Job which face up to the fact of death. And there is Ecclesiastes 3 and the exhortation of chapter 11.

But of course in the face of the fact of death, it is a gospel of hope that we have to proclaim, centred on the death and resurrection of Jesus Christ; and while you will find in the New Testament, as in the Old, questioning about the evanescence of life, as in James 4:14, you will also find there the trumpets of assurance which you must sound to rally your people. I am thinking of the great words of the gospel as we find them, for example, in John 11:25 and John 14. Also the proclamation of immortality as in I Corinthians 15 or Philippians 3 or I Peter 1.

Nor should you neglect great visionary passages like Hebrews 11:1-12:2, in which there is an appropriate text in the very first verse, and another in the thirteenth, as well as yet another in the opening verses of chapter 12.

You should not neglect the first letter of John which is specially appropriate to the witness and memory of particularly loving and lovable people. There is also the ascription with which the book of Jude ends.

And do not despise, because of its very oriental imagery, the comfortable words of the book of Revelation. Both you and your congregation should have enough poetry in you to recognise the truth of vision, and when we have said all that can be said of our hope of heaven, we will remember the quotation of St Paul: 'Eye hath not seen, nor ear heard, neither have entered into the heart of man, the things which God hath prepared for them that love him' (I Corinthians 2:9, KJV).

In connection with funeral and In Memoriam services, it is important to maintain your integrity. Whatever you say must stand the test of honesty. If you can say very little in favour of the deceased then that is what you say. It is neither honest nor kind to devote as much time to the merits of a person whose life was not conspicuously meritorious as you can and would wish to do in the case of a person whose virtues were obvious to all. You will be faced with the task of making a memorial tribute to people of very diverse worth. Give to each his or her due, but no more – always remembering to mix your judgment with mercy and commending them to the grace of that God whose property is forgiveness.

And we must also be honest about the extent of our hope of heaven. Here again the last judgment on that is given to Christ and by God's Christ and not by us. It is a great comfort and also gives cause for caution that the parables of judgment suggest that his judgments are surprising (cf Matthew 25:31-46).

And, finally, we must be honest about our agnosticism about the world to come. On the word of Christ, and believing in his saving death and resurrection, we have a sure ground for faith in the life to come. We can point to the evidence for believing that it is a life of continuing and perfected fellowship with those we have loved and with God himself. But we have also to acknowledge that there is much that we do not know and cannot know about life in the world to come. It is beyond our experience.

I know not, I know not,
What joys await us there,
What radiancy of glory,
What bliss beyond compare.

At the end of the First World War, P T Forsyth wrote a small book with the title *This Life and the Next* (New York: Macmillan, 1918). It is a book coloured by the experience of the war and the dreadful slaughter and untimely death of that period. It is a book which A M Hunter describes as a 'seraphic little book'. And there, in the fourth chapter, Forsyth writes: 'There are those who can quietly say, as their faith follows their love into the unseen, "I know that land. Some of my people live there. Some have gone abroad there on secret foreign service, which does not admit of communications. But I meet from time to time the Commanding Officer. And when I mention them to Him He assures me all is well".' (p 44)

There is a hymn in our *Revised Church Hymnary* which was written after Forsyth's day, but which echoes the sense of that passage. It begins:

For those we love within the veil
Who once were comrades of our way
We thank Thee, Lord; for they have won
*   To endless day.*

And it goes on:

O, fuller, sweeter is that life,
And larger, ampler is the air:
Eye cannot see nor heart conceive
*   The glory there;*

Nor know to what high purpose Thou
Dost yet employ their ripened powers,
Nor how at Thy behest they touch
*   This life of ours.*

And there we do well to leave it with reverent agnosticism and with faith.

8

SPECIAL DAYS

IN addition to having to preach on the great Christian festival occasions, you will find throughout the years of your ministry that you will be called upon to preach on a variety of special occasions, both sacred and secular. I confess I am not happy at making the distinction between what is sacred and what is secular. It is only a rather meaningless distinction, since the incarnation implies that the gap between the sacred and the secular has been closed. At the same time care must be taken not to clutter up the Sundays with so many special days, in addition to the outstanding days in the Christian Year, when we celebrate God's mighty acts, that the ordinary ongoing task of expounding the faith and opening up the Bible to your people is crowded out. The minister of one of our great city churches told me once that one of his problems was that he had too many special services: for the Scouts, the Boys' Brigade, the Guides or the Girls' Brigade, the Territorial Army Unit, the Rotarians, the Red Cross, the Masons, the Sports Council, the Orange Order, the Bible Society, the Royal Society for the Protection of Children, Animals, the Countryside, and services for all the special years – the Year of the Child, the International Women's Year, the Year of the Refugee, and so on and so on. The list was endless – so long, indeed, that he felt at times that he had no freedom just to preach the gospel.

This is a problem which is only acute in a few churches, but we all come across it at some time or other. We may be asked if we will have a special group at a morning service, and we have to decide what we are going to do about them. It should not be assumed as a matter of course that every occasion demands a special sermon.

It is sometimes appropriate, especially if the group is a small addition to the normal congregation, to welcome them into the fellowship and to express pleasure at their presence at a convenient point in the service and leave it at that, allowing them to be part of the congregation. On other occasions a little more may be required by way of recognition of their presence, and this might be done at the beginning of the sermon, and thereafter the sermon need not have specific reference to the visiting group. Sometimes you may find that towards the end of the sermon you can point out the relevance of what you have been saying to them and to their organisation and purpose. It seems to me that often what is more important than addressing the members of the organisation directly is that the whole tone and tenor of the service, including the sermon, should be such as indicates that you are aware, as we always should be, of our congregation, its makeup, its needs, and its wavelength – to use contemporary jargon.

This is, I believe, particularly important if the age group is different from the normal age group of your congregation. You must not talk down to young people, but be aware that you are talking to young people, or to old people for that matter, and the form and content of the whole service – praise, lessons, prayers, and sermon – should indicate this awareness. That can be more effective than a direct singling out of a group or organisation, which indeed may be not only unnecessary but even embarrassing.

There are other occasions when you may not have any identifiable group present but on which you have been asked to observe a specific occasion – Mother's Day, or Father's Day, or St Andrew's Day, or United Nations Day, or whatever – and you may imagine that this requires a special service and special sermon. That is not always necessary; it may be sufficient to have a reference to the occasion in the prayers or a mention in passing, if it comes in naturally, in the sermon. Or, occasionally, the event may be an appropriate subject for the Children's Address.

That having been said – and clearly I am of a mind to discourage the excessive use of the regular morning service for so-called special days – there are times, both regular and occasional, which should be observed as special days. These will vary from country to country and from congregation to congregation.

Joseph Gelineau in *The Liturgy Today and Tomorrow* (New York: Paulist Press, 1978) makes a plea for the more imaginative use of special days. He suggests that the liturgy, which is, simply translated, the worship of the people, has become stale and often irrelevant because we are not as sensitive as we ought to be to the rhythm and pattern of contemporary living. He points out – apparent when you think of it – that even the great festivals of Christmas and Easter are times when many of our people are away on holiday, and that there are important moments in the lives of our people that we ignore. He instances, for example, the beginning of the school year, or the ending of the university or college year, and asks why not, where appropriate, a commencement service or a graduation service within the context of a congregation's worship. Both those occasions are family concerns and should also be the concern of the family of God. Passages? Ecclesiastes and Proverbs have many appropriate texts

Most congregations will celebrate either the end of the year or the beginning of the year – not, I hope, on two successive Sundays. Once annually is sufficient, either the end or the beginning of the year, but not both. But not all congregations will celebrate Harvest Thanksgiving, partly because the members of city and town congregations are some steps removed from primary production, and partly because of the trend, mainly but not exclusively Barthian, which discounts the value of natural theology. In the biblical writings that reflect the thinking and the preaching of the early Church, it is remarkable how little of natural theology there is. It may be that this is because Paul was a citizen of no mean city and not a country man, or it may be that so many of the letters in the New Testament are addressed to city congregations. Certainly Pauline allusions to the life of the natural world are not only very rare compared with our Lord's very frequent references to nature and the natural rhythm of the country, but they are brief and stilted when they do occur. In his speech before the Council of the Areopagus at Athens, for example, he refers in very general terms to 'the God who made the world and everything in it', which is about the only reference to the God of the open air that I can find in Paul.

Now I am not very keen on natural theology – Dr Greenfields is a poor theologian – but I am concerned that we should recognise that the lives of many of our people are directly or indirectly shaped and governed by the rhythms and patterns of the natural world. In Britain agriculture is still one of the largest employers of labour, and I suspect that is also true of America, and it is certainly true of Africa. That being so, I would like to see more attention paid to this fact in rural or semi-rural parishes, which after all means most of our parishes. Not only should Harvest Thanksgiving be observed and made an occasion, but this should be done imaginatively. In my first parish, which was a coal-mining parish, we always had, central in the display of the harvest fruits, a huge lump of coal. And in the fishing port in the Northeast of Scotland where I was brought up as a boy, no Harvest Thanksgiving would have been relevant or complete that did not have a fishing net with its corks and larger floats and the contemporary and ancient symbol of the fish. There was always something special also in the service on the Sunday before the fishing fleet left the port to follow the shoals north or south and fish in distant waters, and also on the return of the fleet to its home waters. There have been from time to time Sundays named and set aside to mark other important occasions in the natural year. I have once preached a sermon on Plough Sunday – marking the breaking up of the ground for the seed (the parable of the Sower was the obvious lesson), and more than once I have preached on Rogation Sunday, which, as the name suggests, asks a blessing in faith on the work done, on the seed sown, and the growing crops. When you think of it, there is something more Christian about rogation, asking in faith, than there is about waiting until you see what God has sent you before you thank him for the harvest! Rogation also gives you an opportunity, which would improve the occasion, to preach on intercessory prayer.

An increasing number of congregations observe Labour Day, in Britain usually on a Sunday near to the first of May. Certainly I would commend with Gelineau not an increase in the number of special days so much as a use of special days which have relevance to the life of the congregation, and days which, like Harvest Thanksgiving, recall our interdependence and emphasise the need to recover a doctrine of work and a sense of vocation and responsibility for one another, which is one of the most clamant of our contemporary needs. The fact that the organisation of much of modern industry makes it difficult to have a sense of vocation and responsibility emphasises the need for us, together with our people, to think on these things.

There is a practice, which appears to be on the increase in the Church, of having a member or members of the congregation take part in the services. They may read a quotation from Scripture, or a poem, or a portion of a biography or from a novel or a play. In special services where you have members of the organisation being recognised, this practice might usefully be employed and, where appropriate, extended. Consideration might be given to asking one of them to give a three-minute account of the purpose of their organisation and how they are fulfilling their purpose. If you do this, it is prudent to take a look at what they propose to say a day or two before the service takes place.

Now, after these general notes about the observing of special days, let us look at some particular occasions and see what might be the appropriate theme or themes and suggested lessons or texts. By and large throughout this book the lessons and texts to which your attention is directed are supplementary to the lessons in the lectionary. But you will probably discover that the theme suggested by the lessons in the lectionary and that of the additional lessons or texts which I propose are the same or complementary.

NEW YEAR

The theme for this occasion, whether on the last Sunday of the old year or the first Sunday of the new – but not both – is time: past, present, and future. And as time marches on, so do we *tempora mutantur et nos in illis.* There are many passages which are relevant to this theme. All nine lections in *The Worshipbook* in one way or another, both in the Old Testament and in the New, reflect the Bible's attitudes to the passing of time. There is the splendid passage in Ecclesiastes 3 which you should certainly read on some New Year occasion, even if you do not preach on it. There is also Psalm 90, the first verse of which would be a good text for a sermon on such an occasion. Another text is Isaiah's promise, 'The LORD will go before you, and the God of Israel will be your rear guard' (Isaiah 52:12), with its marvellous picture of a God who is both vanguard and rear guard and also in the middle of the column. He is a God who is already ahead of us, prospecting the way. He has already engaged the enemies that lie in wait. He is also the God who guards us against what lies behind us, old sins with their long shadows, because he is a God whose property is forgiveness. *And* he is also and always the God who is with us step by step. 'Put your hand into the hand of God, this will be better than a light and safer than a known way.' You should not forget on this occasion that, at the turn of the year, many of your people will be thinking of those they have loved who have in the year that is past reached their journey's end.

Don't despise the simple text as, for example, 'Days should speak, and ... years should teach wisdom' (Job 32:7, KJV). Should they? But do they? Or the splendid promise 'as [are] thy days, so shall thy strength be' (Deuteronomy 33:25, KJV). This applies whatever the days may bring and is a promise which is amply supported by other biblical passages and by the witness of the people of God both biblical and post-biblical. There is also that salutary word for this and many other occasions: 'What is your life? It is even a vapour, that appeareth for a little time, and then vanisheth away' (James 4:14, KJV); and the immediate context of that text is also appropriate.

It was reported to me a few years ago that one of my friends had preached a very fine sermon on the first Sunday of the year in a service which was televised from his church. The title of the sermon was all that I got from my informer. It was 'Three Cheers for the New Year'. I had a hunch that there were only three occasions recorded in the Gospels on which our Lord had used the Greek verb translated 'good cheer.' I checked, and I was right. The following year I borrowed his title and preached my own sermon on 'be of good cheer, thy sins be forgiven thee' (Matthew 9:2, KJV); 'Be of good cheer: it is I; be not afraid' (Mark 6:50, KJV); and 'Be of good cheer; I have overcome the world' (John 16:33, KJV). I have no doubt some time you will do the same!

CHRISTIAN UNITY

This is the second of the special days listed in *The Worshipbook*, and it is a theme on which you will preach or to which you will have occasion to refer on other than special occasions. This is pre-eminently a dominical theme, and the *locus classicus* to which you will, I hope, return again and again is the great intercessory prayer in John 17. This was the chapter that John Knox asked his wife to read to him as he was dying. It was, as he himself says, where he first cast his anchor. Here our Lord prays repeatedly for unity (a prayer by one who was against vain repetitions), and not only for the unity of his present disciples but for future disciples, for us. Not only so, but he defines the kind of unity for which he prays: 'As thou, Father, art in me, and I in thee, that they also may be one in us.' Also you have here the purpose of unity: 'That the world may believe' (John 17:21, KJV).

There is material for half a dozen sermons on Christian unity in that chapter. Don't be afraid of the obvious. Most people need to be reminded about some of the obvious things in the Bible, and this is one of them. And I would also urge you not to fudge the issue by talking about spiritual unity, which is too often used as an alibi for not expressing or doing anything about Christian unity.

In some situations it is now possible and valuable to have an exchange of pulpits with a minister or priest of another denomination when you have a special day on Christian unity.

The other lessons in the lectionary, both in the Old and New Testament, are particularly suggestive as a basis for preaching on this theme.

REFORMATION SUNDAY

This special day is not included in the Church of Scotland *Book of Common Order*, and I welcome its inclusion in *The Worshipbook*. By and large our people are not well instructed in the history of the Church, and I would be inclined to use this occasion, possibly at different times, to expound several themes. One would be the continuity of the Church. My former teacher in the field of Church history, Professor G D Henderson, who is the author of several definitive books on presbyterianism, the eldership, as well as on the history of the Church of Scotland, in his book *The Claims of the Church of Scotland* is obviously incensed at the idea that the Church of Scotland begins with the Reformation. He points out that the name *ecclesia scoticana* is found as early as the eighth century, and, more important, the point he is making is that there is continuity in the Church. The Reformers were equally horrified at the notion that they were setting up a new church.

It is only after that point has been established that one goes on to talk about the need of the pre-Reformation Church for reformation. In that connection it is important to be fair, and fairness can often be more assured by quoting descriptions of the state of the Church at that time given by Roman Catholic sources.

This should lead naturally to a statement of what the achievements of the Reformers have been – the recovery of the Bible, the emphasis on the doctrine of the sovereignty of God, and justification by faith. There was also the recovery of a doctrine of human nature which has had profound political, economic, and social consequences. Again, to be fair, something should be said about how the Reformation affected the Roman Catholic Church and, in particular, about the reformation that, however belatedly, is still continuing apace since Vatican II.

That might very well lead on to a coda on the thoroughly Reformed saying, *ecclesia reformata et semper reformanda*, with an application to our own denomination and congregation.

THANKSGIVING AND HARVEST THANKSGIVING

I have taken those two together because historically they are connected.

I was puzzled to find that Harvest Thanksgiving was not included among the special days in *The Worshipbook*. On inquiry I was told that the origin of Thanksgiving goes back to the early days of settlement. It was thanksgiving for the fruits of the labours of the early settlers when they gathered their first crops in a strange land. It only requires a minimum of imagination to realise what an important occasion that was for the first settlers. Like Abraham they had gone out not knowing whither they went, across the sea to a strange land. It was a land of different climate and ecology from the lands they had left. What would grow in this land, in this climate? What pests and diseases that they had never met before would attack them, their animals, and their crops? Those were questions to which they did not know the answers, but the answers were literally a matter of life and death for them and their families. And this was an experience and an adventure that was repeated again and again as they pushed the frontier back across a vast continent. The picture that is seen again and again in old Westerns of the wagon train making its way across the plain, running out of water and food, and gaunt survivors with parched lips and dehydrated bodies with stumbling feet at the end of their tether at last coming across a water hole and hysterically throwing themselves into it, soaking it in through the pores of their skins, is not just a romantic picture. All that represents a reality which lies behind Thanksgiving. At one and the same time Thanksgiving celebrates God's provision and salutes the pioneers and the heritage of heroism and history that is part of the story of America.

You can see why I suggest that Thanksgiving and Harvest Thanksgiving go together. Every Harvest Thanksgiving is a witness to God's provision and to human labour. At every harvest we recognise God's work, and our work with God and our work together. Harvest is the festival of both divine and human co-operation. I recommend this observance, which is not less but all the more necessary in a society which gets its primary products from a tin can or in a nicely wrapped package of cornflakes, and which needs to be reminded that 'the earth is the LORD's and the fullness thereof', and that it is by the goodness of God and the sweat of another's brow that we get our daily bread.

If you do not have a special Labour Day service, the lessons that you would want to get over, and the doctrine of work you might well expound on such a day, are illustrated by the harvest, and the opportunity of driving them home should be seized. Such lessons come naturally at such a time. Work is the rent we owe God for living. It is also imperative that we work together. Work is always co-operation, co-operation with God, co-operation among ourselves, or life is mean, squalid and impoverished.

There should be no difficulty about texts for harvest – you only need to look up a concordance under 'harvest' or 'earth' or 'first fruits'. Our Lord was a country man, and many of the parables have a rural setting and are appropriate to harvest. Don't despise – I repeat myself – don't despise the simple general text: for example, the opening of Psalm 24 which I have quoted; or 'Thou shalt keep ... the feast of harvest' (Exodus 23:15-16, KJV), which is a good text to reintroduce the Harvest Thanksgiving if it has been dropped; or the ancient promise, 'While the earth remaineth, seedtime and harvest, and cold and heat, and summer and winter, and day and night shall not cease' (Genesis 8:22, KJV).

There are, of course, other texts that will occur to you which are not directly related to harvest. There is the word 'Man shall not live by bread alone', quoted by our Lord at the temptation, reminding us that life is more than food. And, in that connection, there is that splendid observation in Genesis 2:9 (KJV): 'Out of the ground made the LORD God to grow every tree that is pleasant to the sight, and good for food.' God is interested in what looks good as well as what tastes good. God is an artist as well as an agriculturist.

There is a conjunction of harvest and a doctrine of work in two parables in particular, the parable of the Labourers in the Vineyard and the parable of the Talents. Both are difficult parables – all the more reason why you should tackle them. There is work seen as a curse in Genesis 3:19.

What do you say to your people if there has been a disastrous harvest or, for that matter, at any time of disaster? There is a great brave word at the end of that little known book, Habbakuk. One of the finest of the Scottish paraphrases has turned the passage into verse form (Paraphrase 32):

What though no flow'rs the fig-tree clothe,
  though vines their fruit deny,
The labour of the olive fail,
  and fields no meat supply?

Though from the fold, with sad surprise,
  my flock cut off I see;
Though famine pine in empty stalls,
  where herds were wont to be?

Yet in the Lord will I be glad,
  and glory in his love:
In him I'll joy, who will the God
  of my salvation prove.

... ...

God is the treasure of my soul,
  the source of lasting joy;
A joy which want shall not impair,
  nor death itself destroy.

ALL SAINTS' OR MEMORIAL SUNDAY

I have already in part dealt with the appropriate theme and made suggestions regarding texts and passages in the section on In Memoriam services. But those are personal and particular occasions, and something more general should be said at this point. We are all the beneficiaries of those who have gone before, even while we recognise that the heritage of the past is a mixed blessing. It is important to remember and to recall to the congregation that a saint in the New Testament sense was anyone who had something, however meagre, of the Spirit of Jesus Christ. In common understanding a saint is a person of exceptional holiness. That is not the understanding or the use of the term in the New Testament. Everyone is called to be a saint – witness the address to which the letter to the Romans is sent: 'To all that be in Rome, beloved of God, called to be saints' (Romans 1:7, KJV). In short, saint equals Christian.

All Saints' then is an occasion when the Church on earth remembers the Church in heaven and recognises our unity with those who have gone before us. Naturally we remember most clearly our own loved ones and those who have been our spiritual fathers and mothers. And not only the great ones, but ordinary humble folk who have also fought a good fight and kept the faith and finished the course.

The failure to proclaim the communion of saints, which creedally we profess, has led to heretical views and practices which have arisen out of peoples' hunger for an assurance of continuing communion and fellowship with those who have gone from the Church Militant to the Church Triumphant. This faith and hope is thoroughly Christian and finds picturesque expression in Hebrews 11 and is summarised in Hebrews 12:1-2. There is also the great Petrine doxology, and Revelation is a source book for this theme.

While this hope in its fullness belongs to the New Testament, you will also find suggestive passages and texts in the Old Testament and not least in some of the narrative passages. There is David at the cave of Adullam pouring out in dedication to God the water of the well of Bethlehem brought by the three mighty men. This passage has many applications, and one of them is appropriate to this day. A less well known passage that is worth pondering is 2 Samuel 2:18-28, which deals with the tragedy and futility of war, the death of the young man Asahel who was 'as swift of foot as a wild gazelle'. There is the reluctance of the soldier Abner, who finally in despair and exasperation thrust him right through and killed him. There is the soldiers' requiem: 'And all who came to the place where Asahel had fallen and died, stood still.' And, finally, there is the resolution to be reconciled. This is a passage which does not glorify war, and the deglorification of war is something which we must always apply ourselves to. We have to emphasise our Lord's hard command in the Sermon on the Mount.

WORLD COMMUNION

As I understand it, this special day arose out of the world mission of the Church and the ecumenical movement. We do not find it listed in the *Book of Common Order*, but I expect the intention of this day is expressed there by the inclusion of Missionary Sunday. I prefer the term 'World Communion', if only because Missionary Sunday has the implication that mission is something extra and something foreign. Increasingly we are beginning to realise that mission here, there and everywhere is the normal business of the Church, and that increasingly we have to undertake this together, interdenominationally and internationally. It seems to me that there is an overlap in theme between World Communion and Christian unity, but the two observances may be complementary in the sense that Christian unity without World Communion might suggest that it would be nice and cosy if we could get together, whereas World Communion suggests that we get together to go out together. When a World Communion service ends with holy communion, an appropriate text is the caution in I Corinthians 11:29 about 'discerning the Lord's body'. There the reference to the Lord's body is to the Church, the Body of Christ. One of the most encouraging signs in the Church in the last decade has been that the ecumenical movement has ceased to be solely a matter of high ecclesiastical consultation and has become a matter of congregations belonging to different denominational traditions getting together, working, witnessing, and worshipping together. On such occasions it is appropriate to remind the congregation positively that in the beginning of the Church it was when that varied group of disciples were of one accord in one place that they were fired with the Spirit and the Church grew. And, negatively, we should ponder our Lord's word that if you come to worship and there is something between you and your brother, your first duty is to go and be reconciled to your brother. Any reading of Acts and the epistles demonstrates two things: one is how early and how easily the Church could become divided; and the other is the horror, anger, and dismay with which the divisions were regarded. The basic question to a divided Church is: How can this be? Is Christ divided? World Communion should lay upon the hearts and consciences of our people the grievous scandal of our divisions. This ought to be a major concern.

NATIONAL AND CIVIC SERVICES

The story is told about a little boy, son of a minister who had accepted a call from a congregation in Glasgow. The night before they left their country parish the little boy finished his bedtime prayer with the words, 'Good-bye, God, we're going to Glasgow tomorrow'. You can change the name of the city to Edinburgh or Birmingham or Baltimore to suit your audience! But there is a point to the story. Too many people think of the city and the things of the city as God-forsaken and imagine that God has nothing to say, and the Church and the minister therefore have nothing to say, about civic or national affairs. The faith is only for the individual, and preferably for the individual in a community of some idyllic country place. Now, while I doubt very much if God ever intended us to live in the modern multimillion conurbations that cities have become since the Industrial Revolution, the idea that God has nothing to say to men and women as nationals of a country or citizens of a city is to ignore and to deny much of the Word of God contained in the Scriptures of the Old and New Testaments. There, in the Old Testament, God speaks through his prophets not only to individuals but to Israel, to the Jews in their varying situations, in Egypt, in the wilderness, in Canaan, in the promised land, to the United Kingdom of Israel and Judah and to the separate kingdoms. And in the New Testament we find the Church being established in the centres of population in the Mediterranean world, in Rome and Corinth, in Ephesus and Philippi. Again and again our Lord, we are told, addressed 'the people'. He had a word for the community as well as for the individual.

There is therefore good biblical precedent for ministers of the word to speak on national and civic issues. Of course, as always, it is important that ministers who do so should not only know what they are talking about, but should have something more to say than is being said by the media. There is nothing more tedious than a sermon on a topical subject which is merely an echo of what is being said and said better by a good newspaper or television commentator. We have to be sure of our facts, and we have to be clear that the point of view from which we observe and comment on the facts is God's point of view. The prophet's preface was not: 'This is what I think.' It was: 'Thus saith the Lord.' And if you are to speak with that note, you will have the humility to remember there were and are many false prophets, and even the best of the prophets were sometimes wrong.

There are national and civic occasions when you will have an opportunity and a duty to speak to your congregation; and the Word of God being, as I have indicated, addressed to the individual in community and to communities as a whole, there is ample biblical material to draw on.

Biblical generalisations provide wide scope for the preacher. 'Blessed is the nation whose God is the Lord' (Psalm 33:12). 'Where there is no vision, the people perish' (Proverbs 29:18, KJV). 'Except the Lord build the house, they labour in vain that build it: except the Lord keep the city, the watchman waketh but in vain' (Psalm 127:1, KJV). 'The Lord reigneth; let the people tremble' (Psalm 99:1, KJV). And 'The Lord reigneth; let the earth rejoice' (Psalm 97:1, KJV). These are only a few examples that come to mind, and there are many others.

You will find particular biblical circumstances and instances often seem especially relevant to you and to your congregation on occasions, and that some words spoken or observation made in those situations are peculiarly fitting to the people and community which you are addressing. This is where your general background reading into the context and text of the Old and the New Testaments is most helpful. It may help you to avoid panic situations when some sudden and unexpected event happens in the community or in the nation or in the world which you cannot ignore, and in which people will expect a word from the Lord through you. True, the general word, as I have said, may be the appropriate word: 'Comfort ye, comfort ye my people, saith your God' (Isaiah 40:1, KJV) may be the most you can do. 'Cast your burden on the LORD, and he will sustain you' (Psalm 55:22) may be the promise to which you must direct them. But the Bible is rich in great and meaningful incidents which can be applied effectively and relevantly to civic and national services. As early as Genesis there is Abraham going out from Ur of the Chaldees seeking a city which has foundations whose builder and maker is God. There is Jacob, not only at Bethel on the well-known first occasion when he realised for the first time that there is a communication between earth and heaven, between God and us, and his response to that revelation; but there is also Jacob's return to Bethel in Genesis 35 and in a situation of dire trouble both in the family and in his community. Don't miss the context of his return which is given in the previous chapter. There is Samuel – not the infant Samuel, about whom we have all heard, but Samuel the Judge, about whom we ought to know more. Note his farewell speech to the people in I Samuel 12 and the secret of the integrity of the man hidden in I Samuel 7:17 – his home and home community of Ramah; his work – there he judged Israel; his altar – his place of worship, and not for himself only but for his fellows. This is a moving tribute to a great man. Perhaps appropriate at a Memorial Service for a good person.

There is Nehemiah, surveying the ruined city, counting the

cost, and calling everybody to lend a hand, at the point where they are, to mend the walls. There are many strikingly appropriate texts and lessons in that rather neglected book which can inspire a people in a different age and with different problems, yet facing a similar breakdown of civilisation, to rise and build.

There is a great incident in II Kings 5, where the reluctant and proud Naaman, a Syrian, comes to Elisha to be cured of his disease and is told to go and wash seven times in Jordan. His reaction has become a proverbial saying – 'Are not Abana and Pharpar, the rivers of Damascus, better than all the waters of Israel.' That is a defective patriotism. There is material for another sermon in his request for a little bit of the Holy Land – 'two mules' burden of earth' – and his plea for forgiveness for his compromising and bowing down in the house of Rimmon. What did Elisha's response to that mean? There are two and possibly three sermons in that chapter – the third on the greed of Gehazi.

There are the great social prophets like Amos who have still a word of God to say to our careless society.

In the New Testament there is the incident when our Lord saw the city and wept and spoke his word of longing and of disappointment. But remember, in his great commission he adds the word 'beginning from Jerusalem' (Luke 24:47).

It is important on civic and national occasions not to present yourself or the Church as standing in a holier-than-thou relationship to civic and government authorities. In a democracy especially, we are members one of another, and 'we' and 'they' and 'us' and 'them' are not appropriate words. We are in it together. Together we are part of the world's curse or cure. We ought not to be judgmental. Above all we should remember what lay behind our Lord's weeping over Jerusalem. It was an attitude of deep concern and compassion. In all our speaking to the world, we must keep in the forefront of our minds and in our hearts the Gospel word: 'God so loved the world, that he gave his only begotten Son, that whosoever believeth in him should not perish, but have everlasting life.' And not least should we remember how that word continues: 'God sent not his Son into the world to condemn the world; but that the world through him might be saved.' It is on that note that we end.

9

CONCLUSION

IN the Introduction we looked at the evolution of the Christian Year and we followed briefly a historical sketch of how it developed over the centuries. We saw how it had become cluttered with saints' days and how, by the time of the Reformation, Holy Days had been secularized, sometimes to a scandalising extent. As a consequence of this, and as an example of what could be described as the Church's recurrent tendency to throw out the baby with the bathwater, the Reformers deplored the keeping of special seasons and days, even Christmas Day. And while there is clear evidence from Church records that the prohibition was not completely observed, the Puritan influence of the Westminster Confession period re-emphasised the views of the Reformers, and the recovery of the Christian Year and its good intention, which was to direct the attention of the faithful to the mighty acts of our redemption, was delayed. This was especially so in Presbyterian Scotland, and because of the Puritan and not least the Scottish influence it has had a similar effect in America until comparatively recent times.

In America, also, the mobile society of the early days of settlement – a period which lasted up to and into the beginning of this century, in which the slogan was 'Go west, young man', and in which almost everything, good or bad, is attributed to the ever-receding frontier – undoubtedly had an effect. The effect was inimical to consecutive preaching and teaching. The peripatetic preacher, preaching to a different congregation every other Sunday, had little opportunity and less incentive to follow a lectionary or to lead his people gently into the mysteries of the incarnation or the world mission of the Church, or to the way of the cross and the resurrection and the coming of the Holy Spirit. And so you had an emphasis on subjective preaching, on the episodic rather than the systematic, on the inspirational rather than the didactic, on the immediate impact of preaching rather than the cumulative effect of sustained teaching through preaching over a long period. This is not to decry the value of the episodic and the inspirational, but it does explain why there has been such a delay in the general adoption of the practice of using, without being a slave to, a lectionary, and the comparative lack of any wholehearted following of a scheme of preaching which fits in with the Christian Year. There are many signs that this delay is being overcome, and the reluctance to accept the discipline of the Christian Year is rapidly disappearing. My expectation is that both in Scotland and in America by the end of this century we will have more systematic preaching and worship which will be more closely related to the mighty acts and be a fuller witness to a more complete gospel. You who will be preachers and leaders of worship into the twenty-first century will have a part to play in that movement.

It was in that expectation that I have devoted the main body of this book on preaching through the year to Advent, Epiphany, Lent, Holy Week, Easter and Pentecost – in other words, to the main events of the Christian Year. I thought it might be helpful to add two chapters on what might loosely be described as preaching on other sacred and secular occasions, though I have a thoroughly biblical dislike for any suggestion that you *can* divide the sacred and the secular. The plain fact is that there are so many occasions that there was material for more than one chapter. And even two chapters do not exhaust all the occasions on which you will have to preach and conduct public worship.

In this final chapter I want to make some general observations and suggestions regarding both preaching and the conduct of public worship, and I begin with the service as a whole.

It is the custom, especially in America, to have in addition to a text for a sermon a sermon topic or title. What is not so customary is to have a consistent theme for the service, so that the service has a detectable unity from beginning to end. It is important that this should be so. The choice of hymns should not be left to the organist. The organist is a colleague in the ministry and should be consulted about the praise and should have some idea of the 'tone' of the service. It is not exactly helpful if in a service where you are preaching on the sombre subject of sin, the anthem is a joyous caroling of carefree praise. When that happens the fault is yours. You are responsible for the whole service.

At the same time you have to remember if, for example, you are giving to God in a sermon the glory due to his name, that there almost certainly will be in your congregation some who are burdened and heavy-laden and sad at heart. Always remember such in your prayers in the service. And while most of the hymns should be appropriate to the occasion of the service, it is not necessary that all of them should be so. Variety is not only the spice of life, it gives life to a service. Unity in a service does not mean a dull uniformity.

Perhaps a word of caution about humour in a service is more necessary in an American rather than Scottish context. In a Scottish service it is rare to hear a congregation laugh. People may, if you make an exceptionally witty remark, inadvertently allow a slight expansion at the corners of their lips which they suppress as quickly as possible in order to resume the normal funereal expression considered appropriate to public worship. It has always struck me as a curious contradiction that one of the favourite praises of Scottish congregations is Psalm 100. They seem to enjoy singing with a lugubrious air ...

All people that on earth do dwell,
Sing to the Lord with cheerful voice
Him serve with mirth, His praise forth tell,
Come ye before Him and rejoice.

It took me something like ten years to get my last congregation to laugh outright, and even then one of my members apologised to me afterwards for doing so.

On the other hand, there is a tendency both among congregations and ministers in America to think that a service has not been a good one unless there have been at least three laughs in it. You should know and ponder Kierkegaard's parable in this connection. It is about a fire in a circus. The circus manager had a cubicle overlooking the ring. He saw the flicker of flames as he was talking to one of the performers who was waiting to go on. As he dashed to phone the fire brigade he shouted to the man to go and tell the audience to get out. As the flames were spreading the man came back. 'I can't move them,' he said, 'I've gone around the rim of the ring twice. I've told them to get out, the tent's on fire. They just laugh.' The messenger was one of the clowns.

If you are gifted with a sense of humour, thank God for it. It can be an asset in the ministry – and not just or mainly in the pulpit – but use it with great restraint in the house of God. And whatever you do, don't play it just for laughs.

I have already mentioned that much of your preparation for preaching should be indirect rather than direct. I mean by that that you should read widely in classical and modern literature. Don't think that your education in the arts at school or in college ends there – though I think you will be happily surprised to find how many useful quotations or illustrations come from books and plays that you *had* to read in the upper classes in high school or at college. Keep your literary cupboard stocked up and don't think you are wasting your time by reading the latest novel or biography or by going to a currently successful film or play or musical.

I am not a particularly methodical person, but some people find it helpful to have a Commonplace Book in which they note down some impression that a passage in a book has made on them, or some impact that a film or play has had, or some illustration for a sermon that has occurred to them from something seen or heard. All that I have been able to do in that way is to have a large stiff envelope marked on the outside – 'On the Stocks' – into which goes a haphazard collection of such things, plus possible suitable texts for a sermon on some future occasion, which I have noted when reading the Bible, usually with a scribbled outline for the sermon. Much of this material I may never use, but the practice I have found has its uses, and not least in that it allows ideas to have a gestation period, so that when the delivery time approaches the thought has hopefully matured.

One of the problems of the ministry as a vocation is that it demands a very high degree of *self*-discipline. You seldom have a boss looking over your shoulder. Your kirk session is not going to supervise you. Even in a multi-ministerial team, where there is a leader other than yourself, the leader is not going to direct everything you do, and is certainly not going to spend time constantly overseeing you. And, if the day comes, as come it will, when you are the leader, even if it is a leader of a ministry of one, there is only One above you, and that is God whose servant you are. And he is not going to supervise and chivy you. He has more to do. That places a very great responsibility on you as an individual. You must always be aware of that. You are directly responsible to God. You must not be haunted by that sense of responsibility, nor daunted by it, but if you are not to become either careless or driven into a frenzy of activity by a sense of guilt and inadequacy, you must face up to your responsibility both to God and to the people whom he has given into your charge.

How do you face up to the responsibility of the ministry with its so varied and inordinate demands? You have to be an administrator. You have to be a fund-raiser. You have to be a pastor and a counsellor. You have to be an organiser. You have to be a teacher. You have to be a preacher. You have to be good with children. You have to get alongside the teenagers. You have to be the friend of young couples. You have to understand the pressures of the middle-aged. You have to look after the aged. You have to rejoice with those entering on matrimony. You have to exclaim over the newborn babe. You have to comfort those who mourn. You have to prepare those who are about to die. Who is sufficient for these things? Our sufficiency is of God.

The first point to make is simply this: if you are responsible to God you must at the beginning of each day give time to waiting for your instructions. You must wait upon God. You will not get a list of what you have to do, though in my experience it is surprising how detailed sometimes God's instructions are. 'Do this' ... 'Go and visit so-and-so' ... 'Here is how you must begin to tackle this problem, that difficult situation or person.' Now, I am not saying that a voice will speak in your ear, but I am saying that you will, if you wait upon God, go out with a confidence that comes from the faith that you have asked him to be with you, and he has said he will, and he keeps his promise. He who promised is faithful. And the note of your morning prayer is not so much: 'Lord, what am I to do?', but rather: 'Lord, what would *you* have me do?' It is good to have a set course of Bible reading, and preferably one which some of your people are also following. Looking back on my ministry, which some people would count both varied and effectual, I am very conscious that my greatest failure was in this matter of personal devotion, private prayer, and Bible study. And my ministry suffered because my own soul was not being nourished as much as it ought to have been by this regular waiting upon God.

You too will be pressured to cut it short, to scamp it. You too will be tempted to use the time of private prayer for preparing the public prayers for your services and your Bible study as a part of the preparation for your sermon, but that is to allow your professionalism to crowd out your personal devotional life, and it is your professional duties which will suffer. You *are* a professional, and you have to be as scrupulous and meticulously professional as a doctor or teacher or lawyer or any other professional person. But you are, first and foremost, a witness of God, and you must walk daily with him if you are to be both his servant and his friend, and if you are to be a true witness of God to your people. It is that and that above all which will save you from being merely a skilled or slick professional.

You cannot preach about an unknown God. You can teach a theology or theologise, but you can't proclaim and be the herald of a God whom you do not know. And you can only know God by being intimate with him, by keeping company with him.

One of the problems that you have to face as a minister is that it is very difficult to be systematic with regard to your work. In addition to leading your people in worship and preaching, you will have pastoral duties, visiting your members and, as far as possible, your parish, and prospective members. I made it a rule during my ministry never to visit anyone outside my parish unless I had seen them regularly attending church. You will have sick visiting, and you will have to comfort those who mourn. You will have to prepare people for the baptism of their children and for confirmation; and while in large congregations this may in part be done collectively, it should always also be done individually. You will have important and less important administrative tasks, from organising the organisations to keeping a record of your expenditure on postage. You will also bear in mind your ordination vows and take your due part in the work of the presbytery, synod, and General Assembly and their committees. And you will get more of this to do as you get older. You will also be expected to serve on the committees of local good causes, especially causes connected with education and health. As a trained speaker you will be invited from time to time to give addresses and to speak to all kinds of organisations, and my advice to you is not to be too scintillating as an after-dinner or any other kind of speaker outside the church, or you will find that this can take up more time than it merits. I have known ministers who boasted that in one January they had delivered more than a dozen Immortal Memories to Robert Burns. Even if it was one Immortal Memory delivered twelve times, it was eleven too many.

You must establish your priorities early, and you must learn to say no. You must also try to organise your day systematically, even if the system is more ideal than real, and whatever happens to the rest of the day you should have a set time for being in your study to begin the day's work. One professor of Practical Theology taught that you should not go into your study in your slippers. Be shod for the job. Certainly the idea behind that advice was good. Dress for your work even if you do wear an old jacket while you're working at your desk. It is not my business to advise you about keeping records of visits, or about filing systems, or how to administer and organise the varied work of your congregation, but it may be of some use to you to know how I set about preparing a service.

I begin on a Tuesday morning with one or two scrap sheets of paper. If I am preaching one of a series of sermons I put down the title of the sermon and I think about a passage from Scripture appropriate to the theme. I might find it – and usually this happens – in one of the lessons in the lectionary for that Sunday. I note it, and then look to see what I have on my shelves by way of commentary on the passage. And I look the passage up in the commentary. It is important to do this at an early stage, for you may discover sadly that your initial interpretation is wrong, and you may have to look for another and more appropriate text and passage. You should also by this stage have some idea of how much of the context of the text you are going to give to the congregation, and, later, how best you can make the context interesting and relevant.

By the way, I would advise you against buying one set of commentaries. Sets of commentaries vary in value according to the expertise of the individual commentator. I might qualify that by saying that you might have one reputable series of commentaries, but you should buy individual commentaries from different series as they appeal to you, or as they are favourably reviewed. You certainly want at least one compendium commentary on the Bible so that you have some kind of cover for every book in it; but that by itself, while very useful, is hopelessly inadequate.

That might be enough work on a sermon for one morning.

On the following morning the shape of the sermon should begin to emerge. This matter of shape is very important. If the sermon is shapeless it tends to be a rambling disconnected affair; and while you may, and on occasion will, ramble on engagingly, if you make this your practice your congregation will cease to follow you because they will sense that you are not going anywhere. Get down the points you want to make first, and then see how you can work them into a sequence. You may find that once you have got your points down the order in the finished sermon is not necessarily the order which you thought of first. In my experience it is usually at this stage that illustrations or cross references to other biblical passages, to a saying of Jesus, or a parable, or an incident, or a poem, or a lesson from biography comes to mind and may have to be searched out. It should be jotted down before you forget it. Better to have it down and not use it than recall it after you have preached the sermon because you failed to put it down when it occurred to you.

You will also find as you are going about your business during the week that incidents, conversations, something on television or in the newspaper will become grist for your mill and relevant to your sermon. This is not because you will always be consciously looking for such material – better not to do that – but, because you have the theme of your sermon in mind, the illustrative matter will sometimes subconsciously emerge.

One of the advantages of starting as early as Tuesday morning is that you should have time to let the sermon simmer. Whenever I have had to begin writing a sermon before it was finished, it has invariably turned out half-baked. I seldom sit down to write a sermon which I do not finish at a sitting unless I am interrupted. And it is very rare for me to preach a sermon which I have not written out in full, although it is even rarer for me to preach exactly what I have written. In order to be able to write the sermon in full at a sitting, I have to have all my quotations from books written out on the scrap paper and my desk cleared of commentaries and other books that I may have consulted. It is distracting and time-consuming to be jumping from your manuscript to a book and back again to the manuscript. It is also one of the main reasons why sermons sometimes appear 'bitty' and do not flow. Patchwork is fine for quilts, but it has a soporific effect in sermons.

During this process of the growth of the sermon it is useful to have a box in the corner of your scrap paper in which you have mapped out the Order of Service; or you may have a separate sheet on which, when the content of the sermon is taking shape, you can write appropriate opening and closing hymns if such occur to you. For these and for the remainder of the hymns you may be guided by the sections in the hymnbook and, in the Church of Scotland, by the suggested praise for each Sunday of the year. But the selection of hymns should not be done until you have some idea of what the sermon is about, even if it is only a rough idea. Following the Christian Year also makes it easier for your organist in choosing an anthem. As far as possible the prayers in the service should also be prepared after you have your sermon well in hand. And again it is a good thing to set aside part of one morning in the week, and if possible the same morning each week, for the preparation of the prayers. If you follow some such pattern of preparation, the service should have a unity which otherwise it may lack.

The method of preparation for a service which suits me may not suit everyone, but each preacher should have some method and should give adequate time, and that means a lot of time, to the preparation of the sermon and the service as a whole. It has been my practice to write out everything, and I still continue this practice. I recommend that every minister do this for at least the first ten years; after ten years the habit is likely to be established! That does not mean you must read your sermon word for word, or your prayers, but it is rather a foolish prejudice (now largely gone) to think there is something wrong about a read sermon or read prayers. Much depends on the type of sermon, and even more depends on the type of preacher. If it is a closely argued sermon I will tend to follow my manuscript. In other sermons which have a clearly defined pattern, I may preach from notes which contain little more than the main headings and quotations, and not infrequently I dispense with notes altogether. But it took me years, and failing eyesight, to make me risk the freedom of having no notes at all. It is a freedom attended by risks and the not infrequent annoyance of forgetting to include an apposite illustration or quotation.

But if you are going to read your sermon, read it as one who is speaking to people. Learn to read well. There was a time when read sermons were not acceptable. An old Scotswoman of a former generation was asked what she thought of a young minister's sermon. After a momentary silence her verdict was: 'It was read. It wisna well read. And it wisna worth reading!' If you are going to read, and I can see no reason for not doing so – though you should try preaching from notes after you have written out the sermon – at least learn to read well. Indeed, there is something to be said for reading your sermon aloud in the privacy of your study. You are not writing an essay. You are to be speaking to people.

You cannot preach to people unless you know people, unless you are constantly meeting with them and at as deep a level as they will allow you to meet with them. The preacher who is not a pastor will inevitably be somewhat remote when preaching. That is not to say that you will not feel at times the conflict of demands upon you, the conflict of the demands of people on you as their pastor and the demands of the pulpit from which you must preach. The choice is not an either/or. It is a both/and. You may find some comfort in the evidence in the New Testament that our Lord himself was aware of this pressure and conflict and that from time to time he took himself and his disciples away, apart from the pressure of people. In this too, from time to time, you must follow his example. But you must always care more about people than about preaching. Having said that, I am not suggesting that you should diminish or despise the importance of preaching. 'How are they to hear without a preacher?' (Romans 10:14). You are sent to preach, and it is time we recovered a sense of our high calling to preach the word. I do not despise, nor would I have you neglect other legitimate means of communicating the gospel: through group Bible study, through music and drama, through dialogue and participation of the congregation in worship, as well as through personal witness, pastoral visiting, and counselling – all these are aids to evangelism. But one of the main tasks to which you must give much time and thought and sweat and blood and tears is the preparation of yourself as a preacher.

It is this preparation of yourself that I have been talking about in the main so far, and I would conclude this part of the chapter by expanding a little on the matter of getting away from it all, which, as I have pointed out, our Lord did on occasion. I believe there is great value in going away for the refreshment and recreation of a retreat – for many years I used to go for a week to Iona – or for a refresher course of study; and you should plan to do this in addition to your annual holiday break. Let me emphasise this matter of planning. You must do this about a year ahead. Sit down with your new diary in the dead days between Christmas and the New Year and work out when you are going on retreat or on a refresher course and when you are going on holiday, for if you don't do something like that your diary will get filled up, and you may find that you have the greatest difficulty in getting away at all. And you do this planning with your wife if you are fortunate enough to have one.

You also ought to be scrupulous in setting aside one whole day a week when you are off duty. And make it the same day each week. If you don't you will find yourself being tempted to have a game of golf any day of the week, or to go fishing whenever the mood takes you. Then you really will begin to neglect your work and have a bad conscience about it. It is, as I have found, much better to set aside one day – think of the glorious feeling of martyrdom you can enjoy when, as often happens, some duty comes up that prevents you getting your day off. You owe it to your congregation and to yourself to get away from your work one day in the week. They will respect your right to your day off duty.

You must also devote time to your spouse and family. Ministers' spouses and families are among the most neglected. A minister friend told me that when discussing with his son what he was going to do with his life, he thought he would ask him if he had considered the ministry. The teenager son indicated that that was not one of his options. Father said he would be interested to know why not. 'Because we never see you. You're too busy looking after other people,' was the reply. 'And,' said my friend in some dismay, 'you know there's some truth in that.' There is. I have often thought of the occasion when Jesus was busy with the crowd and they said that his mother and brothers wanted to see him, and Jesus said, 'Here are my mother and my brothers!' (Matthew 12:49). The truth is that as ministers we have another family, the larger family of the congregation, the family of God which we are called to serve. The only hope for us as family members is, as far as we can, to integrate the small natural and the large spiritual family, but we must remember our peculiar and special responsibilities to our small natural family. The Church owes an incalculable debt to the loyalty and love of the spouses and children of its ministers all over the world, without whose willing co-operation this difficult task of uniting the natural and spiritual family could not be achieved. It is a matter of wonder that in so few cases has the integration failed. There is a case for celibacy of the clergy, but the contribution made by the spouses and families of ministers and preachers to the building up of the kingdom of God can hardly be exaggerated.

This has not been achieved without real sacrifice, both economic and spiritual, on the part of a multitude of unknown and unrecognised spouses and their children, who, however, would readily acknowledge that they have indeed obtained in this world through the Church, and richly beyond their friends' imagining, fellowship and advantages which cannot be evaluated, through being taken to the hearts of that larger family which the Church is and which each congregation is intended to express and embody.

Some ministers, through busyness or fear of being thought closer to some of their members than others, are deprived of natural friendships. This is unfortunate for, as much as anyone, and perhaps more than most, we need the stimulus and comfort that come through friendships. Most of us are blessed with the warm friendship of fellow ministers; some of those friendships are formed in our college days and are kept in repair through the years. Some develop through association with neighbouring ministers and fellow presbyters. Such friendships are of great value because fellow ministers have an understanding of the problems of the ministry and the critical situations that can arise and in which we feel the need for advice. Not least do we sometimes need the candid ministerial friend who will deflate our pomposity, modify our temptation to authoritarianism, and generally help us not to think more highly of ourselves than we ought to think. And who will also, when we are discouraged and cast down, give us reassurance and encouragement. And sometimes our need is for far more than encouragement. Dr Johnstone Jeffrey and Dr Edward Jarvis were distinguished ministers of the Church of Scotland in Glasgow – both became moderators of the General Assembly. Dr Jarvis's son was killed in the war. Dr Johnstone Jeffrey read the news in his morning paper and immediately went to see his colleague. He rang the bell. Dr Jarvis opened the door and drew him into the house and said brokenly: 'Come in Jeffrey and be a minister to me. I'm a man without a minister.' At times we *are* without a minister, and at such times we need to be ministered to. We need a minister friend to be a minister to us.

Nor should your friendships be confined to ministerial colleagues. It is perfectly natural that you should have a closer friendly relationship with some of your members than you have with the generality of your congregation. Dr Roderick Bethune succeeded Dr James S Stewart – not once but twice – first at Beechgrove, Aberdeen, and then at North Morningside, Edinburgh. One of his less sensitive members at Edinburgh said to him that he preferred J S Stewart's sermons, and added, 'You don't mind me saying that I like James Stewart better than you'. Roddie put his hand on his shoulder and said reassuringly, 'Not at all. As a matter of fact I like many of my members better than I like you!' This is natural.

Nor should you confine your friendships to members of your congregation. You may find outside your congregation, and indeed outside the Church, folks with whom you have common artistic or recreational interests, interest in music or the arts or literature or fishing or golf or what have you. Not only does that add to your enjoyment of life, but it may also bring into your perspective a point of view other than the 'churchy' point of view, and it may contribute something stimulating and of value to your thinking and your understanding. Our Lord, again and again, is found in the company of the outsider. And sometimes, if we make friends of the outsiders, we may have the joy of seeing them come inside.

We are too inclined as ministers to associate only with those we agree with. This is a mistake. It makes for dullness of mind. I always find that a loch with the liveliest trout is one that has a few pike in it. For those of you who are not fishers, I should add that the pike is a predator and the trout is its prey. You should not confine your *reading* to books that you agree with. That is conducive not only to dullness but to deadness, and the death of the mind and heart will lead to the death of a congregation. If you are liberal in your theology – whatever that may mean – read a book by a good conservative theologian. If you are a conservative theologian – whatever that may mean – read a book by a good liberal theologian. But make sure that the theologian you are reading in any case is in the front rank. It's no use reading an Aunt Sally liberal or conservative theologian or biblical commentator. It is the good ones that stretch your mind and make you mad. The bad ones only confirm what you thought all along and don't stimulate you or make you possibly modify or change your opinion. One of the frightening dangers of the ministry is that our minds become fixed and inflexible. This we must try to avoid. The Holy Spirit is always trying to lead us into new truth.

There is also the opposite danger to which we are exposed, the danger of being too susceptible to and carried away by the latest asylum of thought. Like the Greeks in Athens, we are always inclined to be looking for some new thing, for the latest bandwagon that is rolling by so that we can jump on it. If you marry the trend of the present generation you may be sure you will be a widow in the next.

The surest safeguard against the dangers of inflexibility on the one hand, or of susceptibility to every wind that blows on the other, is to be Christocentric. Jesus Christ is our standard of judgment. It is he who makes all things new. He speaks to us of new birth, of life, terms that imply growth. There are too many stillborn Christians and too few who are constantly growing in grace and in the knowledge of our Lord and Saviour Jesus Christ. At the same time we should keep in mind that he is the same yesterday and today and forever. He is the image of the eternal God, and there is nothing quite so up-to-date as the eternal. It was one of Nelson's captains who said, 'Christ is my compass, he never deviates'. But remember a compass is an instrument that points you in the right direction. It is useful for voyaging, for exploration, for keeping you on the right lines when you are on the move. Christ is our critic, and fortunately for us his judgment is always mixed with mercy and the forgiveness which we need and for which we daily pray.

You will have other critics, and if you are wise you will listen to them and try to evaluate their criticism dispassionately. You should neither resent criticism and thus write it off as irrelevant or unjust, nor be supersensitive and go into a depression every time you receive a hurtful knock, when some pet project is rejected by the kirk session or the congregation, or when some outspoken and disgruntled member tells you what he thinks of something you have said or done and makes clear that he doesn't think much of it. We ministers *have* to be sensitive if we are to be any good at our job, but we must guard against being oversensitive *about ourselves.* That is a form of selfish indulgence, and it can be very disabling. You will almost certainly have times of depression when you doubt if you are any good; you will even have times when you doubt the goodness of God. As to the first doubt, that may not be altogether a bad thing. You may be right! At any rate it is better than an unfounded belief in one's own ability and an overweening conceit or even complacency. A candid spouse is the antidote for that. I liked the cartoon in *Punch* that showed the vicar's wife knitting by the fireside and looking up as her husband enters jauntily twirling his hat in his hand. The caption recording her comment was: 'I gather your sermon on Humility went like a bomb.'

As for doubt about the goodness of God, you can still be in the company of great souls like Job, the psalmists, Thomas and our Lord himself. He understands. Our faith is not that we believe in God. Our faith is in the faithfulness of God. It is in the last resort not our hold on God that matters. It is God's hold on us. There are those two aspects of faith, and they are illustrated by the stone carvings at each side of one of the windows in Iona Abbey. On the one side is the figure of a monkey with its young one clinging fiercely to its back. On the other side of the window is a cat carrying its kitten limply in its mouth. Sometimes, perhaps too often, we feel we have to hang on desperately, we mustn't let go. Sometimes, perhaps too seldom, we have to let go and let God carry us and simply say with Thomas, doubting Thomas, 'My Lord and my God!' Thank God for Thomas!

Always, whether at times of justifiable self-abasement or of unjustifiable self-congratulation, you must remember that 'we have this treasure in earthen vessels', and that indeed any excellency or potency in our words or works is of God and not of us, and to him be the glory.

It is important to remember that the ministry of which Paul speaks is the mission and ministry of the whole people of God. Naturally in this book I have been addressing myself to those in training for the ministry as we think of it in the context of a seminary and to preaching the gospel which is one of the chief tasks of that ministry. But we must realise that our task as ministers of the word and sacraments is to develop in our congregation a sense of their individual and collective ministry as the people of God where they are and in their community. We all have this treasure in earthen vessels, and even the most unlikely can demonstrate – and sometimes the more unlikely the more demonstrative it is – that it is from God alone that anything excellent and effective in building up the kingdom of God comes. Jesus Christ came preaching the gospel of the kingdom of God, and as the Father sent him so he sends us, and in this ministry he has promised to be with us always. In that confidence we go and we preach.

Notes

Book of Common Worship: published in 1993 by Westminster/John Knox
Press (available). This book is based on *The Worshipbook* of 1972 (John
Knox Press). A Software edition of the *Book of Common Worship* is also
available. Contact Westminster/John Knox Press, 100 Witherspoon
Street, Louisville KY 40202-1396 for further details.

Book of Common Order: published in 1994 by Saint Andrew Press (available). The book was published on behalf of the Panel on Worship of
the Church of Scotland. Saint Andrew Press is part of the Church of
Scotland's Board of Communication, 121 George Street, Edinburgh
EH2 4YN.